THE WORLD'S FINEST
CHICKEN

THE WORLD'S FINEST
CHICKEN

RECIPES BY SONIA SLYER & JANICE METCALFE

RECIPE PHOTOGRAPHY BY PHIL WYMANT

GENERAL EDITOR MARGARET OLDS

STEWART, TABORI & CHANG
NEW YORK

Text by Sonia Slyer and Janice Metcalfe
Food photography by Phil Wymant and Travis Trewin
Edited by Margaret Olds and H.D.R. Campbell
Designed by Stan Lamond
Food styling by Ann Creber and Janet Lodge
Nutritional analysis by Carolyn Kelly
Copyedited by Kate Etherington, Heather Jackson, Susan
Page, Melanie Falick and Judith Sutton
Typeset by Suzannah Porter
Index by Diane Harriman
Scenic photographs from the Random House (Australia)
Photo Library

Published in 1996 and distributed in the U.S. by
Stewart, Tabori & Chang
a division of U.S. Media Holdings, Inc.
575 Broadway, New York, NY 10012

Distributed in Canada by General Publishing Ltd.
30 Lesmill Road, Don Mills, Ontario, Canada M3B 2T6

Library of Congress Cataloging-in-Publication Data
Slyer, Sonia
        The world's finest chicken / by Sonia Slyer :
photography by Phil Wymant ; general editor,
Margaret Olds.
        p.   cm.
        Includes index.
        ISBN 1-55670-452-6 (hardcover : alk. paper)
        1. Cookery (Chicken) 2. Cookery, International.
        I. Title.
TX750.5.C45S59 1996
641.6'65—dc20   95-47933
                                CIP

Contributors: Michael Campbell, Sarah Kolberg,
Copeland H. Marks, Nicole Routhier, Amla Sanghvi,
Dolores Simon, Joanne Weir.

Film separation: Pica Colour Separation
Overseas Pte Ltd, Singapore
Printed in Malaysia by Times Offset (M) Sdn Bhd

10 9 8 7 6 5 4 3 2 1

Page 1: *Sea and sky are echoed in the blue dome of a Greek
Orthodox church on the island of Mykonos, Greece.*
Pages 2–3: *People travel for days, sometimes weeks, to attend the
camel market at Nagaur in the Indian state of Rajasthan.*
Page 4: *Colorful boats pack historic Camogli harbor in the Gulf
of Genoa, Italy.*
Pages 6–7: *Russia, a land of stark climatic contrasts, displays
one of its many moods.*
Pages 8–9: *A conglomeration of shape and color in Taxco,
southern Mexico.*

Contents

Introduction

CHICKEN is a universally enjoyed food. Apart from its intrinsically delicious flavor, it is so versatile, easy to prepare and nutritious. The recipes found in this book have been selected from traditional favorites from around the world and then adapted for today's healthier lifestyle. However, we have not compromised on the authentic flavors and hope you will enjoy these recipes as much as we did in the test kitchen!

For many centuries recipes were passed down through generations, often orally or through practical demonstrations, while individual preferences subtly altered the recipes. Today mass communication and travel have brought these traditional ways of cooking age-old dishes out of their homelands and into the kitchens of every adventurous cook. In time this will lead to the creation of new "traditional" recipes, with each country contributing its own special blend of flavors.

India, where the domestication of the jungle fowl over four thousand years ago is believed to have led to the chicken of today, has given the world a cuisine that is rich in spice and heat. These same spices—pepper, ginger, turmeric, cilantro, and cumin among others—also play a vital role in the cooking of Thailand, Indonesia and Vietnam, yet the dishes produced in those countries are quite different from the dishes of India. Japanese cuisine took on and adapted much of the complexity of the Chinese approach to cooking but remained quite distinct. Italy, Spain, France, Greece, Lebanon, and Morocco all border the Mediterranean Sea, yet all have their own distinctive cuisines—for example, dairy products are treated differently. Cheese is often married with chicken in

Opposite: In Russia the land is very important—here the farmhouse has been abandoned but the land is still tended.

Moroccan shops like this one offer an intriguing range of wares to tempt passing shoppers.

Japan's sacred mountain, Mount Fuji, provides a stunning background for these simple buildings.

France and Italy, while yogurt is used in conjunction with chicken in Greek, Arabian and North African dishes. The United States is a classic example of a cuisine melding many influences, with the indigenous spices and vegetables from the New World treated in a recognizably Old World manner.

In many countries chicken used to be eaten only on special occasions, but with modern breeding methods it has become more affordable in most countries.

Some of the recipes are quite high in fat in their original form—these have been adapted to reduce the fat as far as is compatible with retaining the authentic flavors. The nutritional analysis for each recipe includes the amount for total fat as well as for the different types—the saturated fat level is the most critical in health terms.

In general, the current trend in healthy balanced diets is to cut back fat intake, particularly the saturated fats. These fats are responsible for much of the cholesterol that can constrict the arteries. Chicken has a higher proportion of polyunsaturated fats and fewer saturated fats than most red meats. By removing the skin before cooking the chicken, the fat reduction per serving is significant. Where the flavor or method of cooking the chicken requires the skin to be left on, those on a strict diet may remove the cooked skin before eating the chicken.

A 3½ oz (100 g) serving of cooked chicken meat provides 1 oz (28 g) of first quality protein. It also supplies many of the B complex vitamins, especially niacin, vitamin B_{12} and pantothenic acid.

The lush green hillside of Valldemosa, on the Spanish island of Majorca.

Brightly-clothed people and the occasional tree add life and color to the Great Indian Desert.

Zinc is an essential mineral found mostly in the dark meat of chicken, as are other valuable minerals including magnesium and potassium.

Chicken is also a good source of the iron that our bodies need to make the hemoglobin that enables red blood cells to carry oxygen through the body. This particular iron is easily absorbed and women in particular need a regular supply of easily absorbed iron in their diets to help prevent anemia and associated problems.

This collection of recipes ranges from the simple to the exotic, from mild to hot and spicy, from everyday meals to rich and lavish. Importantly, the dishes have been designed for today's busy lifestyle, and the techniques simplified.

We hope you enjoy this book, a collection of new "traditional" recipes.

SONIA SLYER and JANICE METCALFE

Chicken Congee

CHI'CHU

SERVES 6

1 cup (7 oz/210 g) short-grain
   rice
3 cups (24 fl oz/750 ml) water
3½ cups (28 fl oz/875 ml)
   chicken stock, skimmed of fat
½ cup (4 fl oz/125 ml)
   Chinese rice wine
5 thin slices ginger
½ teaspoon salt
¼ teaspoon freshly ground
   white pepper
4 cups (1 lb/500 g) diced
   cooked chicken

SIDE DISHES

shredded preserved cabbage
pickled Chinese lettuce
soy sauce
Chinese hot bean paste
   (chili bean paste)
cilantro (coriander) leaves
scallions (spring onions), sliced

Rice is the staple food of the Chinese, and this porridge-like rice soup is eaten for breakfast as well as at other times of day. The flavor of the soup is enhanced by the side dishes, some of which are only available from Chinese food stores.

PREPARATION   *5 minutes*
◆ Wash the rice under cold running water until the water runs clear, then drain.

COOKING   *45 minutes*
◆ Combine the water, half of the stock, the wine, ginger, salt and pepper in a medium-sized saucepan. Add the rice and stir thoroughly.
◆ Bring to a boil, then reduce the heat and simmer, stirring frequently, until the rice mixture has a porridge-like consistency, about 30 minutes.

◆ Stir in the remaining stock and the diced chicken. Heat through and serve immediately with side dishes of your choice.

PER SERVING (ANALYSIS EXCLUDES SIDE DISHES)
246 calories/1028 kilojoules; 20 g protein; 3.7 g fat, 14% of calories (1.2 g saturated, 4.4% of calories; 1.8 g monounsaturated, 6.9%; 0.7 g polyunsaturated, 2.7%); 28 g carbohydrate; 0.8 g dietary fiber; 313 mg sodium; 1.2 mg iron; 58 mg cholesterol.

A tranquil rural landscape in China; life in country areas has changed little over the centuries.

Chicken Congee

Chicken Soup with Cellophane Noodles

SOTO AYAM KUNING

SERVES 4

7 oz (220 g) cellophane noodles
1 lb (500 g) chicken breast fillets
1 onion, sliced
¼ cup celery leaves
2 bay leaves
1 teaspoon salt
1 teaspoon black peppercorns
4 cups (32 fl oz/1 l) water
2 teaspoons vegetable oil
2 garlic cloves, finely chopped
1 in (2.5 cm) ginger, grated
1 small red chili, thinly sliced
1 teaspoon finely chopped
    lemongrass
½ teaspoon ground turmeric
½ cup (1 oz/30 g) bean sprouts
4 scallions (spring onions), finely
    chopped
2 hard-boiled eggs, chopped

Also called bean threads, cellophane noodles are made from mung beans. Rice noodles can be used in this recipe if cellophane noodles are unavailable. Both rice noodles and cellophane noodles need to be soaked in hot water before using.

PREPARATION   *15 minutes*
◆ Soak the noodles in hot water for 10 minutes. Drain and cut into 2 in (5 cm) pieces.

COOKING   *30 minutes*
◆ Place the chicken, onion, celery leaves, bay leaves, salt and peppercorns in a large saucepan. Add the water and bring to a boil. Reduce the heat and simmer until the chicken is cooked through, about 20 minutes.
◆ Remove the chicken and cut into bite-sized pieces. Strain the stock and reserve. Wipe out the saucepan.
◆ Heat the oil in the saucepan over medium-high heat. Add the garlic, ginger and chili and cook, stirring

continuously, for 2 minutes. Stir in the lemongrass and turmeric and cook, stirring continuously, for 1 minute.
◆ Return the chicken and stock to the saucepan, and bring to a boil. Add the noodles and bean sprouts and cook, stirring occasionally, for 3 minutes.
◆ Garnish with the scallions and hard-boiled eggs and serve.

PER SERVING
260 calories/1090 kilojoules; 23 g protein; 5.4 g fat, 19% of calories (1.5 g saturated, 5.3% of calories; 2.4 g monounsaturated, 8.4%; 1.5 g polyunsaturated, 5.3%); 29 g carbohydrate; 0.7 g dietary fiber; 444 mg sodium; 1.7 mg iron; 110 mg cholesterol.

Indonesian meals usually end with fresh fruit—this market in Yogyakarta shows a small selection of the abundance available.

Chicken Soup with Cellophane Noodles

Chicken and Chickpea Soup

CALDO TLALPENO

This soup has its origins in Tlalpán, now a suburb of Mexico City. It contains an unusual mixture of ingredients, including the indigenous avocado and chili and the introduced radish and cheese.

SERVES 6

1 vine-ripened tomato
3 canned, hot green chilies
4 cups (32 fl oz/1 l) chicken stock, skimmed of fat
8 oz (250 g) chicken breast fillets
1 tablespoon vegetable oil
1 small onion, finely chopped
1 garlic clove, crushed
1 cup (6½ oz/200 g) cooked chickpeas
1 ripe avocado
4 radishes, thinly sliced
6 scallions (spring onions), finely chopped
½ cup (1½ oz/45 g) freshly grated sharp cheddar cheese

PREPARATION   *15 minutes*

✦ Place the tomato in a bowl and cover with boiling water. Let stand until the skin begins to split, about 10 minutes. Remove the tomato from the water, peel and chop.
✦ Place the chilies and a ½ cup of the chicken stock in a blender and purée.

COOKING   *50 minutes*

✦ Place the remaining stock and the chicken in a large saucepan and bring to a boil, then reduce the heat and simmer for 20 minutes.
✦ Remove the chicken with a slotted spoon and set aside to cool. Set the saucepan with the stock aside.
✦ Heat the oil in a small, non-stick skillet over medium-high heat. Add the onion and garlic and cook until the onion is soft, about 3 minutes. Add the tomato and cook until it is soft and most of the liquid has evaporated, about 5 minutes.

✦ Stir the tomato mixture and the chili mixture into the saucepan containing the stock. Bring to a boil over medium heat, then simmer for 5 minutes.
✦ Meanwhile, shred the chicken.
✦ Stir in the chicken and chickpeas and simmer for 5 minutes.
✦ Meanwhile, slice the avocado. Divide the radishes and scallions among 6 bowls.
✦ Spoon the soup into the bowls and garnish with the sliced avocado and grated cheese. Serve immediately.

PER SERVING
263 calories/1102 kilojoules; 18 g protein; 18 g fat, 59% of calories (5.8 g saturated, 18.9% of calories; 8.2 g monounsaturated, 27.1%; 4 g polyunsaturated, 13%); 9 g carbohydrate; 3.6 g dietary fiber; 483 mg sodium; 1.6 mg iron; 33 mg cholesterol.

Chicken and Corn Soup

SOPA DE POLLO CON ELOTE

Corn (or maize) has been cultivated in Mexico for thousands of years and features prominently in the country's mythology, religion and cuisine. It is cooked in a variety of ways and is also ground into a flour known as *masa harina*.

SERVES 6

2 vine-ripened tomatoes
12 oz (375 g) boneless, skinless chicken thighs (thigh fillets)
3 cups (24 fl oz/750 ml) chicken stock, skimmed of fat
1 onion, sliced
1 stalk celery, chopped
1 teaspoon coriander seed
½ teaspoon black peppercorns
½ teaspoon salt
2 cups (12 oz/375 g) fresh, frozen (thawed) or canned corn kernels
cilantro (coriander) leaves, for garnish

PREPARATION   *15 minutes*

✦ Place the tomatoes in a bowl and cover with boiling water. Let stand until the skin begins to split, about 10 minutes. Remove the tomatoes from the water, peel and chop.

COOKING   *35 to 40 minutes*

✦ Place the chicken, chicken stock, onion, celery, coriander seed, peppercorns and salt in a large saucepan. Bring to a boil, reduce the heat, cover and simmer until the chicken is cooked through, about 20 minutes.
✦ Remove the chicken fillets with a slotted spoon and set aside to cool.
✦ Strain the stock into a bowl and discard the solids.
✦ Return the stock to the saucepan and add the corn

and tomatoes. Bring to a boil. Cover, reduce the heat and simmer for 10 minutes if using fresh corn, 5 minutes if using canned or frozen.
✦ Meanwhile, shred the chicken.
✦ Return the chicken to the saucepan and simmer for 3 minutes. Pour into 6 warm soup bowls, garnish with the cilantro leaves and serve with corn bread.

PER SERVING
147 calories/616 kilojoules; 17 g protein; 2.1 g fat, 13% of calories (0.6 g saturated, 4% of calories; 1 g monounsaturated, 6%; 0.5 g polyunsaturated, 3%); 15 g carbohydrate; 2.8 g dietary fiber; 382 mg sodium; 1 mg iron; 29 mg cholesterol.

Chicken and Chickpea Soup

Tortilla and Chicken Soup
SOPA DE TORTILLA A LA MEXICANA

SERVES 6

2 vine-ripened tomatoes
4 corn tortillas
2 tablespoons vegetable oil
1 onion, finely chopped
4 jalapeño chilies, finely chopped
6 cups (48 fl oz/1.5 l) chicken
    stock, skimmed of fat
4 cups (1 lb/500 g) cooked
    shredded chicken
2 tablespoons freshly squeezed
    lime juice
salt, to taste

In Mexico, tortillas are made at home on a griddle called a *comal* made of metal, or, more traditionally, clay. Being one of the country's staple foods, they are prepared daily in most households.

PREPARATION   *15 minutes*
◆ Place the tomatoes in a bowl and cover with boiling water. Let stand until the skins begin to split, about 10 minutes. Remove the tomatoes from the water, peel and chop.
◆ Cut the tortillas into ½ in (1 cm) strips.

COOKING   *25 minutes*
◆ Heat 1 tablespoon of the oil in a large saucepan over medium-high heat. Add the onion and chilies and cook until the onion is soft, about 3 minutes.
◆ Add the chicken stock and bring to a boil. Stir in the shredded chicken. Reduce the heat and simmer for 10 minutes.

◆ Stir in the tomatoes and lime juice. Check the seasoning and add the salt if desired. Simmer for an additional 5 minutes.
◆ Meanwhile, heat the remaining oil in a medium-sized skillet over medium-high heat. Add the tortilla strips and cook, stirring, until crisp.
◆ Ladle the soup into 6 bowls and serve, accompanied by the tortilla strips.

PER SERVING
261 calories/1094 kilojoules; 27 g protein; 12 g fat, 40% of calories (3 g saturated, 10% of calories; 4.2 g monounsaturated, 14%; 4.8 g polyunsaturated, 16%); 12 g carbohydrate; 1.6 g dietary fiber; 622 mg sodium; 1.4 mg iron; 107 mg cholesterol.

Chicken Soup
CALDO DE POLLO

SERVES 4

1 avocado
1 teaspoon freshly squeezed
    lemon juice
6 cups (48 fl oz/1.5 l) chicken
    stock, skimmed of fat
10 oz (300 g) chicken
    breast fillets
8 oz (250 g) thin spaghetti
2 serrano or jalapeño chilies,
    finely chopped
1 teaspoon salt
4 lime slices

This soup, known as *sopa aguada* (literally wet soup, with a liquid consistency), is served at the start of the meal. *Sopa seca*, dry soup, is the result of rice or other foods absorbing the liquid in which they are cooked, and follows the *sopa aguada*.

PREPARATION   *10 minutes*
◆ Cut the avocado into dice, and sprinkle the lemon juice on top.

COOKING   *35 minutes*
◆ Place the chicken stock and chicken fillets in a large saucepan. Bring to a boil, then reduce the heat and simmer, covered, until the chicken is cooked through, about 20 minutes.
◆ Using a slotted spoon, remove the chicken from the saucepan and set aside.
◆ Stir in the spaghetti, chilies and salt and simmer until the spaghetti is just tender, about 7 minutes.

◆ Meanwhile, dice the cooked chicken. Return it to the saucepan and cook for an additional 2 minutes.
◆ Divide the avocado among 4 warm bowls, then ladle the soup on top. Serve immediately, topped with a slice of lime.

PER SERVING
448 calories/1877 kilojoules; 27 g protein; 16 g fat, 33% of calories (3.9 g saturated, 7.9% of calories; 9.6 g monounsaturated, 19.8%; 2.5 g polyunsaturated, 5.3%); 47 g carbohydrate; 4.3 g dietary fiber; 1056 mg sodium; 1.6 mg iron; 38 mg cholesterol.

Chicken and Coconut Milk Soup

TOM KHA GAI

SERVES 4

*2 chicken breast fillets,
  about 4 oz (125 g) each*

4 stalks lemongrass

*3 cups (24 fl oz/750 ml)
  chicken stock, skimmed of fat*

*2 cups (16 fl oz/500 ml)
  coconut milk*

*4 small red chilies, seeded and
  finely sliced*

*¼ cup (2 fl oz/60 ml) freshly
  squeezed lime juice, plus
  extra if required*

½ teaspoon fish sauce

*1 tablespoon thinly sliced
  galangal*

*2 kaffir lime or lime leaves, torn
  into pieces*

Thai soups are usually served along with the rest of the meal, not as a separate course, but this is satisfying enough to stand on its own as a light meal. This creamy, aromatic dish is one of the best known of all Thai soups.

PREPARATION   *15 minutes*

✦ Cut the chicken into bite-sized pieces.

✦ Cut the lemongrass into 2 in (5 cm) lengths and crush them with a rolling pin.

COOKING   *25 to 30 minutes*

✦ Place the stock and coconut milk in a large saucepan and mix well. Add the lemongrass and bring to a boil.

✦ Reduce the heat to medium and add the chilies, lime juice, fish sauce, galangal and kaffir lime leaves.

✦ Simmer until the chicken is cooked through, about 15 to 20 minutes. Check the seasoning, and add extra lime juice if a more tart taste is desired.

✦ Ladle into individual soup bowls and serve.

PER SERVING

284 calories/1190 kilojoules; 18 g protein; 19 g fat, 61% of calories (16.2 g saturated, 52% of calories; 1.9 g monounsaturated, 6%; 0.9 g polyunsaturated, 3%); 9 g carbohydrate; 0.7 g dietary fiber; 307 mg sodium; 0.6 mg iron; 31 mg cholesterol.

*Clearing
the land for
agriculture in
rural Thailand.*

*Chicken and
Coconut Milk Soup*

Chicken Liver Terrine

TERRINE AU FOIE DE VOLAILLE

SERVES 8

7 oz (220 g) chicken livers
1½ cups (3 oz/90 g) firmly
packed dry bread crumbs
11 oz (345 g) ground
(minced) chicken
2 garlic cloves, crushed
1 teaspoon black peppercorns
1 tablespoon brandy
1 tablespoon port
1 tablespoon chopped oregano
1 tablespoon chopped
flat-leaf parsley
1 tablespoon chopped rosemary
1 large egg, lightly beaten
4 slices (rashers) lean bacon

A terrine is a deep baking dish usually made from earthernware or porcelain. It has also given its name to the dishes cooked in it. Terrines need to be made at least 24 hours in advance to allow the flavors to mingle and mature.

PREPARATION   *20 minutes*

◆ Preheat the oven to 375°F (190°C).
◆ Coarsely chop the livers. Place in a bowl with the bread crumbs and knead until the mixture forms a ball. Add the chicken, garlic, peppercorns, brandy, port, herbs and egg and combine well.
◆ Line the sides and base of a large terrine or loaf pan (9 × 5 × 3 in/25 × 15 × 6 cm) with the bacon slices. Spread the liver mixture evenly over the bacon and cover with a tightly fitting lid or aluminum foil.

COOKING   *1 hour and 20 minutes*
plus overnight refrigeration

◆ Place the terrine in a baking dish and add enough hot water to the baking dish to come 2 in (5 cm) up the sides of the terrine. Bake for 1¼ hours. Remove the lid, carefully pour off any fat, cover and refrigerate overnight.
◆ Serve with toast.

PER SERVING
232 calories/969 kilojoules; 25 g protein; 8.1 g fat, 31% of calories (2.9 g saturated, 11.2% of calories; 3.4 g monounsaturated, 13%; 1.8 g polyunsaturated, 6.8%); 13 g carbohydrate; 0.8 g dietary fiber; 746 mg sodium; 3.8 mg iron; 171 mg cholesterol.

An ornate balcony, typical of the town of Sospel in the South of France.

Chicken Liver Terrine

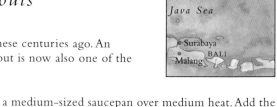

Chicken Breasts with Bean Sprouts

AYAM ISI TAUGE BUMBU BALI

Bean sprouts were introduced to Indonesia by the Chinese centuries ago. An important ingredient in Chinese cooking, the bean sprout is now also one of the most commonly used vegetables in Indonesian cuisine.

SERVES 6

4 chicken breast fillets, about
    4 oz (125 g) each
8 oz (250 g) ground (minced)
    chicken
1/3 cup (1/2 oz/15 g) bean sprouts
2 small red chilies, seeded and
    finely chopped
2 teaspoons vegetable oil

SAUCE

2 teaspoons sesame oil
2 small red chilies, seeded and
    finely chopped
2 green chilies, seeded and finely
    chopped
1 garlic clove, finely chopped
1 stalk lemongrass, thinly sliced
1 large tomato, peeled and chopped
1 cup (8 fl oz/250 ml)
    coconut milk
1 teaspoon ground coriander
1 teaspoon palm or brown sugar
1/2 teaspoon shrimp paste

PREPARATION   *25 minutes*

✦ Preheat the oven to 350°F (180°C).
✦ Place the chicken fillets between 2 sheets of plastic wrap and flatten to an even thickness with a meat mallet, taking care not to make any holes in the flesh.
✦ Combine the ground chicken, bean sprouts and red chilies in a medium-sized bowl. Place one quarter of the stuffing over the bottom narrow edge of each fillet, roll up and secure with a toothpick.

COOKING   *1 hour*

✦ Use a pastry brush to brush the chicken rolls with the vegetable oil. Wrap each roll in aluminum foil and place on a baking sheet. Bake until the chicken is cooked through, about 25 to 30 minutes. Cool in the foil for about 10 to 15 minutes.
✦ Meanwhile, make the sauce. Heat the sesame oil in

a medium-sized saucepan over medium heat. Add the chilies, garlic, lemongrass and tomato and cook, stirring, until the chilies are soft, about 5 minutes. Stir in the coconut milk, coriander, sugar and shrimp paste, reduce the heat and simmer until thickened, about 5 minutes. Place the sauce in a blender and blend to a smooth consistency.
✦ Cut each chicken roll into 3 slices. Arrange the slices on a serving dish and pour the sauce on top. Serve with rice noodles.

PER SERVING

250 calories/1047 kilojoules; 29 g protein; 13 g fat,
46% of calories (7.2 g saturated, 25.3% of calories;
3.6 g monounsaturated, 12.9%; 2.2 g polyunsaturated, 7.8%);
4 g carbohydrate; 1 g dietary fiber; 82 mg sodium; 1.4 mg iron;
71 mg cholesterol.

Chicken in Banana Leaves

AYAM PEPES

Banana leaves impart a subtle fragrance to the chicken and add to the presentation of this dish. Look for banana leaves and powdered coconut milk in specialty Asian food stores. If banana leaves are unavailable, use several layers of foil.

SERVES 4

8 banana leaves
1 onion, halved
1 small lemon, peeled, coarsely
    chopped and seeded
1 in (2.5 cm) ginger, coarsely
    chopped
1 garlic clove
2 small red chilies, halved and
    seeded
1/4 cup chopped cilantro (coriander)
1/4 cup shredded coconut
2 tablespoons powdered
    coconut milk
1/2 teaspoon ground cumin
1/2 teaspoon garam masala
1/4 teaspoon ground fenugreek
2 teaspoons virgin olive oil
4 chicken breast fillets,
    about 4 oz (125 g)

PREPARATION   *30 minutes*

✦ Bring a large stockpot of water to a boil, dip the banana leaves briefly into the boiling water. Set aside.
✦ Finely chop one half of the onion.
✦ Place the lemon, the remaining half onion, the ginger, garlic, chilies and cilantro in a blender and purée until smooth. Transfer to a small mixing bowl and stir in the shredded coconut, powdered coconut milk, cumin, garam masala and fenugreek.

COOKING   *50 minutes*

✦ Heat the oil in a small, non-stick skillet over medium heat. Add the finely chopped onion and cook until golden, about 5 minutes.
✦ Add the purée, reduce the heat to low and cook, stirring occasionally, for 3 minutes.

✦ Remove from the heat, then spread the mixture evenly over the top of the chicken fillets.
✦ Wrap each fillet in 2 banana leaves tying with raffia or twine, then wrap securely in aluminum foil.
✦ Place the parcels on a steaming rack. Steam over simmering water for 25 to 30 minutes.
✦ Remove the foil wrappers and serve the chicken in the leaf parcels with rice.

PER SERVING

217 calories/910 kilojoules; 29 g protein; 9.6 g fat,
40% of calories (5.2 g saturated, 21.6% of calories;
3.5 g monounsaturated, 14.4%; 0.9 g polyunsaturated, 4%);
3 g carbohydrate; 1.9 g dietary fiber; 75 mg sodium; 1.2 mg iron;
63 mg cholesterol.

Chicken in Banana Leaves

Chicken Satay

SATAY AYAM

MAKES 8

1 lb (500 g) chicken breast fillets
3 tablespoons soy sauce
2 tablespoons freshly squeezed
   lemon juice
1 teaspoon palm or brown sugar
1 small onion, finely chopped
½ teaspoon chili powder
8 wooden skewers

PEANUT SAUCE

2 teaspoons peanut oil
2 teaspoons finely chopped
   red chilies
1 garlic clove, crushed
1 cup (8 fl oz/250 ml) water,
   plus extra if required
⅓ cup (3 oz/90 g) crunchy
   peanut butter
2 tablespoons freshly squeezed
   lemon juice
2 tablespoons soy sauce
2 teaspoons palm or brown sugar

Indonesia's delicious satays are often served with a tasty peanut sauce—increase the amount of chilies for an even spicier flavor. The traditional cooking method is over coals, so this dish is also a good choice for grilling outdoors.

PREPARATION   *10 minutes plus*
                        several hours marinating time

◆ Cut the chicken into ¾ in (2 cm) cubes.
◆ Combine the soy sauce, lemon juice, sugar, onion and chili powder in a large mixing bowl. Add the chicken pieces, stirring well to coat. Cover and marinate in the refrigerator for several hours.
◆ Soak the skewers in cold water for at least 30 minutes to prevent them from charring during cooking.
◆ Preheat the broiler (grill).

COOKING   *20 minutes*
◆ To make the sauce, heat the oil in a small saucepan over medium-high heat. Add the chilies and garlic and stir-fry for 30 seconds. Reduce the heat to low, add the water and peanut butter and cook, stirring continuously, until well mixed. Remove from the heat and stir in the lemon juice, soy sauce and sugar. If the sauce is too thick to pour, stir in a little extra water. Pour into a small bowl for serving and set aside.

◆ Thread the chicken pieces onto the skewers, reserving the marinade in the refrigerator. Place under the hot broiler and cook, basting frequently with the reserved marinade, until golden brown on both sides, about 3 to 4 minutes per side.
◆ Serve the satays with the peanut sauce, accompanied by steamed rice.

PER SATAY (INCLUDES PEANUT SAUCE)
127 calories/533 kilojoules; 17 g protein; 5.6 g fat, 39% of calories (1.3 g saturated, 9% of calories; 2.6 g monounsaturated, 18%; 1.7 g polyunsaturated, 12%); 3 g carbohydrate; 1 g dietary fiber; 550 mg sodium; 0.8 mg iron; 31 mg cholesterol.

Carrying produce across a bridge on Ceram, one of the original Spice Islands, now known as the Moluccas.

Green Enchiladas with Chicken

ENCHILADAS VERDES

MAKES 8

SAUCE

1 tablespoon virgin olive oil

1 large onion, chopped

2 jalapeño chilies, chopped

15 oz (470 g) canned tomatillos, chopped

3 tablespoons chopped cilantro (coriander)

½ cup (4 fl oz/125 ml) chicken stock, skimmed of fat

8 corn tortillas

3 cups (12 oz/375 g) shredded, cooked chicken

1 cup (3 oz/100 g) freshly grated, sharp cheddar cheese

1 small onion, finely chopped

The tomatillo, the basic ingredient of this green sauce, is a small, green vegetable that resembles a tomato and has a distinctive acidic flavor. Tomatillos are available either fresh or in cans from specialty stores. Make the salsa one day in advance.

PREPARATION *50 minutes plus several hours refrigerating time*

◆ To make the sauce, heat the oil in a small, non-stick skillet over medium-high heat. Add the onion and chilies and cook until the chilies are soft, about 3 to 5 minutes. Add the tomatillos, reduce the heat and simmer, stirring occasionally, for 5 minutes. Transfer the mixture to a food processor and process until puréed. Place the purée in a small saucepan, add the cilantro and chicken stock and simmer for 30 minutes. Pour into a bowl, cool, cover and refrigerate for several hours or overnight.

COOKING *40 minutes*

◆ Place each tortilla in a medium-sized, dry, non-stick skillet over medium-high heat, and cook, turning once, just until soft, about 30 seconds on each side.

◆ Preheat the oven to 350°F (180°C).

◆ Place the sauce in a medium-sized, non-stick skillet and warm over low heat. Remove from the heat. Dip a tortilla in the tomatillo sauce, then place on a plate. Sprinkle with one-eighth each of the chicken, cheese and chopped onion. Roll up the tortilla and place seam down in a roasting pan. Repeat with the remaining tortillas. Pour any remaining sauce on top.

◆ Bake until heated through, about 15 minutes.

PER SERVING

267 calories/1116 kilojoules; 19 g protein; 15 g fat, 52% of calories (6.4 g saturated, 22% of calories; 6.7 g monounsaturated, 23%; 1.9 g polyunsaturated, 7%); 15 g carbohydrate; 2.5 g dietary fiber; 214 mg sodium; 1.2 mg iron; 79 mg cholesterol.

Local markets in Mexico carry a variety of fresh produce.

Chicken in Pasta Shells

POLLO CONCHIGLIE

SERVES 6

1 cup (4 oz / 125 g) chopped, cooked chicken, skin and fat removed
¾ cup (2 oz / 60 g) button mushrooms, sliced
1 garlic clove
1 tablespoon chopped basil
1 tablespoon chopped flat-leaf parsley
2 teaspoons chopped oregano
¼ teaspoon freshly ground black pepper
1 small red chili, seeded
2 teaspoons freshly squeezed lemon juice
1 large egg
1 teaspoon virgin olive oil
36 conchiglie (large pasta shells)
1¼ cups (10 fl oz / 300 ml) Italian tomato sauce
¼ cup (1 oz / 30 g) freshly grated Parmesan cheese
basil sprigs, for garnish

Conchiglie means seashells, and so seashell-shaped pasta shells are known as *conchiglie*. In this traditional appetizer from southern Italy, the pasta shells are filled with a tasty chicken stuffing, topped with a tomato sauce and baked.

PREPARATION   *15 minutes*
♦ Combine the chicken, mushrooms, garlic, basil, parsley, oregano, pepper, chili, lemon juice and egg in a food processor. Process until finely chopped.
♦ Preheat the oven to 375°F (190°C).

COOKING   *50 minutes*
♦ Bring a large saucepan of salted water to a boil. Add the oil and the pasta shells and cook for 5 minutes. Remove from the heat, drain the pasta and rinse under cold running water to stop the cooking process.

♦ Spoon the chicken mixture into the pasta shells. Arrange the pasta shells in a baking dish, pour the sauce on top and sprinkle with the Parmesan cheese. Bake until hot and bubbling, about 35 minutes.
♦ Serve hot, garnished with the basil sprigs.

PER SERVING
134 calories / 559 kilojoules; 11 g protein; 5.3 g fat, 36% of calories (2.2 g saturated, 15.1% of calories; 2.4 g monounsaturated, 16.2%; 0.7 g polyunsaturated, 4.7%); 10 g carbohydrate; 1.6 g dietary fiber; 624 mg sodium; 0.9 mg iron; 62 mg cholesterol.

Art and religion are part of everyday life in Italy; this apartment building in Rome displays a painting of the Madonna and Child.

Chicken in Pasta Shells

Chicken Pastry Rolls

DJAJ B'AJEEN

Phyllo pastry is often regarded as quintessentially Greek, but it is also widely used in Middle Eastern cooking. Phyllo pastry is difficult and time-consuming to make, but it can be purchased either fresh or frozen from many supermarkets.

SERVES 8

2 tablespoons (1 oz / 30 g)
    unsalted butter, melted
½ cup (2 oz / 60 g) pine nuts
2 teaspoons virgin olive oil
1 large onion, finely chopped
4 cups (1 lb / 500 g) finely
    chopped, cooked chicken
¼ cup chopped raisins
¼ teaspoon ground allspice
pinch ground cinnamon
½ teaspoon salt
¼ teaspoon freshly ground
    black pepper
2 tablespoons finely chopped
    flat-leaf parsley
16 sheets phyllo pastry
herb sprigs, for garnish

**CUCUMBER AND YOGURT
DRESSING**
¼ cup peeled and chopped cucumber
½ cup (4 oz / 125 g) low-fat
    plain yogurt

PREPARATION   *15 minutes*
✦ Lightly grease a baking sheet with a little of the melted butter.

COOKING   *1 hour*
✦ Toast the pine nuts in a dry, large, non-stick skillet over low-medium heat, stirring continuously, until golden, about 3 minutes. Transfer to a plate.
✦ Heat the oil in the skillet over medium heat. Add the onion and cook until soft, about 3 minutes. Add the chicken, raisins, allspice, cinnamon, salt and pepper and cook, stirring, for 3 minutes. Remove the skillet from the heat and stir in the parsley and pine nuts. Let cool for 15 minutes.
✦ Preheat the oven to 400°F (200°C).
✦ While working with the phyllo pastry, keep the unused sheets covered with a damp cloth.
✦ Brush 1 sheet of the pastry with a little of the melted

butter. Place a second sheet on top and brush with a little butter. Then place ¼ cup of the chicken mixture slightly above the bottom edge of the pastry. Fold in the sides, roll up firmly and place, seam side down, on the baking sheet. Continue in this manner until all the pastry and filling have been used. Bake until golden, about 15 minutes.
✦ Meanwhile, combine the cucumber and yogurt in a small bowl.
✦ Garnish the pastry rolls with the herb sprigs and serve with the cucumber and yogurt dressing.

PER SERVING
273 calories / 1142 kilojoules; 23 g protein; 11 g fat, 36% of calories (4.4 g saturated, 14.4% of calories; 5 g monounsaturated, 16.2%; 1.6 g polyunsaturated, 5.4%); 21 g carbohydrate; 1 g dietary fiber; 411 mg sodium; 1.4 mg iron; 96 mg cholesterol.

Chicken and Pistachio Croquettes

KAFTA DJAJ

Nuts are a popular ingredient in the cuisines of the Middle East, used in both sweet and savory dishes. Pistachios are believed to have originated in the region around Lebanon, and have been cultivated there for thousands of years.

SERVES 6

3 large eggs
12 oz (375 g) ground (minced)
    chicken
1 cup (4 oz / 125 g) fresh
    bread crumbs
6 tablespoons chopped pistachios
1 teaspoon ground coriander
1 teaspoon ground cumin
½ teaspoon ground cinnamon
½ teaspoon ground turmeric
1½ tablespoons finely chopped
    flat-leaf parsley
¾ cup (1½ oz / 45 g) toasted
    bread crumbs
¼ cup (1 oz / 30 g) all-purpose
    (plain) flour
2 tablespoons vegetable oil
cucumber and yogurt dressing
    (see recipe above)

PREPARATION *30 minutes plus 2½ hours refrigerating time*
✦ Lightly beat one of the eggs in a large bowl, then add the chicken, fresh bread crumbs, 4 tablespoons of the pistachios, spices and parsley. Refrigerate for 2 hours.
✦ Combine the toasted bread crumbs and remaining pistachios for the coating.
✦ Lightly beat the remaining eggs in a shallow bowl.
✦ Divide the chicken mixture into 12 portions and shape each into a ball. Roll each ball in the flour, dip in the beaten eggs, then roll in the bread crumb mixture. Refrigerate the prepared croquettes for 30 minutes.

COOKING   *15 minutes*
✦ Heat the oil in a large, non-stick skillet over medium heat. Add the croquettes and cook, in 2 batches if

necessary, turning occasionally, until golden all over, about 5 to 7 minutes per batch.
✦ Garnish with herb sprigs and serve with the cucumber and yogurt dressing on the side.

PER SERVING
157 calories / 657 kilojoules; 11 g protein; 8.5 g fat, 48% of calories (1.7 g saturated, 9.6% of calories; 3.4 g monounsaturated, 19.2%; 3.4 g polyunsaturated, 19.2%); 9 g carbohydrate; 1.1 g dietary fiber; 106 mg sodium; 1.1 mg iron; 67 mg cholesterol.

*Chicken Pastry Rolls (top) and
Chicken and Pistachio Croquettes*

Chicken with Egg and Lemon Sauce

KOTOPOULO AVGOLEMONO

SERVES 8

*1 roasted or barbecued chicken,
    about 3 lb (1.5 kg)*
4 large eggs
juice of 2 lemons

Avgolémono (egg and lemon) is perhaps better known in the famous Greek soup, *soupa avgolémono,* but it also features as a sauce for fish or vegetables. Here it is used in an appetizer that is light, fragrant and tangy.

PREPARATION   *25 minutes*
✦ Cut the chicken into serving portions, cover and refrigerate.
✦ Separate the eggs and place the egg whites in a large mixing bowl. Using a whisk, beat the egg whites until they are frothy. Beat in the egg yolks until well mixed. While beating, add the lemon juice a drop at a time, and continue beating until the sauce has a creamy, frothy consistency.

COOKING   *8 minutes plus 20 minutes cooling time*
✦ Place the sauce in a small saucepan and stir continuously over very low heat until it begins to thicken and coats the back of a spoon, about 3 to 5 minutes. Remove from the heat; the sauce will continue to thicken on standing. Cool to room temperature, about 20 minutes.
✦ Pour the sauce on top of the chicken and serve on a bed of mixed salad greens.

PER SERVING
*162 calories/676 kilojoules; 22 g protein; 7.5 g fat,
42% of calories (2.7 g saturated, 15.1% of calories;
3.6 g monounsaturated, 20.2%; 1.2 g polyunsaturated, 6.7%);
0.5 g carbohydrate; 0.6 g dietary fiber; 85 mg sodium; 1 mg iron;
171 mg cholesterol.*

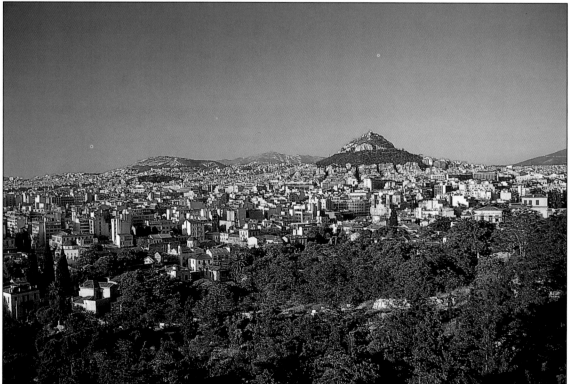

*The sunlit
skyline of
Athens.*

Nakhon
Sawan
Nakhon
Ratchasima
Lop
Buri
BANGKOK
Thon
Buri
Chon Buri

Galloping Horses

MAH HAW

MAKES 60

26 oz (820 g) canned lychees
1 tablespoon sesame oil
1 garlic clove, crushed
1 small red chili, finely chopped
2 cilantro (coriander) roots,
    finely chopped
7 oz (220 g) ground (minced)
    chicken
1 tablespoon fish sauce
1 teaspoon sugar
1 tablespoon shredded cilantro
    (coriander)
1 cucumber, sliced
cilantro (coriander) leaves,
    for garnish

The tropical lusciousness of the lychee is perfectly complemented by the slightly spicy filling. Fresh lychees can be substituted if available. This dish is always known as "galloping horses" but the reason for this intriguing name is not known.

PREPARATION   *25 minutes*
✦ Cut the lychees in half.

COOKING   *35 minutes*
✦ Heat the oil in a wok over medium heat. Add the garlic and chili and cook, stirring, for 1 minute. Add the cilantro roots and cook for 30 seconds.
✦ Add the chicken and cook, stirring and breaking up any lumps, until cooked through, about 5 minutes.
✦ Stir in the fish sauce, sugar and shredded cilantro leaves, and cook for 2 minutes. Transfer the chicken mixture to a plate and let cool for 15 minutes.

✦ Place the cucumber slices in a single layer on a serving platter. Spoon the chicken mixture into the lychee cavities and place the filled fruit on top of the cucumber slices. Garnish with the cilantro leaves, and serve.

PER 2 STUFFED LYCHEE HALVES
24 calories/ 103 kilojoules; 2 g protein; 0.7 g fat, 32% of calories (0.2 g saturated, 9% of calories; 0.2 g monounsaturated, 9%; 0.3 g polyunsaturated, 14 %); 3 g carbohydrate; 0.3 g dietary fiber; 15 mg sodium; 0. 2 mg iron; 5 mg cholesterol.

Traditional costumes are worn for many of Thailand's festivals; this woman is from northern Thailand.

Chicken Satay

GAI SATAY

Satays are popular all over Southeast Asia. Originally from Indonesia, they were introduced to Thailand from Malaysia to the south and have become a favorite Thai dish. They make a delicious appetizer served with the peanut dipping sauce.

MAKES 12

12 wooden skewers
1 lb (500 g) chicken breast fillets

MARINADE

5 tablespoons (2½ fl oz/75 ml)
  coconut milk
2 tablespoons soy sauce
1 tablespoon vegetable oil
2 teaspoons ground turmeric
1 teaspoon curry powder
½ teaspoon ground coriander
½ teaspoon ground cumin

PEANUT SAUCE

2 teaspoons peanut oil
2 teaspoons red curry paste
2 teaspoons fish sauce
2 teaspoons lemon juice
¼ cup (2 oz/60 g) crunchy
  peanut butter
½ cup (4 fl oz/125 ml) coconut
  milk

PREPARATION   *20 minutes plus at least 1½ hours*
✦ Soak the skewers in water for at least 30 minutes to prevent charring during cooking.
✦ Cut the chicken lengthwise into thin strips and thread onto the skewers.
✦ Mix together all the marinade ingredients.
✦ Place the chicken skewers in a single layer in a large dish. Pour the marinade over and marinate for at least 1 hour, or overnight, in the refrigerator, turning once.
✦ Just before cooking, preheat the broiler (grill).

COOKING   *15 minutes*
✦ Broil the chicken, occasionally brushing with the marinade, until cooked through, about 5 minutes per side.

✦ Meanwhile, prepare the peanut sauce. Heat the oil in a medium-sized, non-stick saucepan. Stir in the red curry paste, then the remaining ingredients, reduce the heat to low and cook, stirring, for 3 minutes.
✦ Serve the chicken with the warm peanut sauce on top, or in a small bowl on the side for dipping.

PER SATAY (INCLUDES PEANUT SAUCE)
133 calories/557 kilojoules; 12 g protein; 8.9 g fat, 59 % of calories (4.1 g saturated, 27.1% of calories; 2.7 g monounsaturated, 17.7%; 2.1 g polyunsaturated, 14.2%); 2 g carbohydrate; 1 g dietary fiber; 301 mg sodium; 1.2 mg iron; 21 mg cholesterol.

Deep-Fried Spring Rolls

CHA GIO

The Thais tend to eat snacks like these spring rolls all through the day. They are delicately flavored and are often served with a mildly sweet but spicy cucumber dipping sauce. They are ideal as an appetizer or as finger food.

MAKES 24

⅓ cup (3 fl oz/90 ml) white
  wine vinegar
¼ cup (2 oz/60 g) sugar
½ teaspoon salt
1 small red chili, finely chopped
4 oz (125 g) cellophane noodles
1 small cucumber, finely chopped
1 egg white
1 tablespoon cold water
2 teaspoons sesame oil
5 oz (150 g) ground (minced)
  chicken
2 garlic cloves, finely chopped
2 oz (60 g) button mushrooms,
  finely chopped
1 tablespoon fish sauce
1 tablespoon soy sauce
½ teaspoon sugar
24 spring roll wrappers
vegetable oil for deep-frying

PREPARATION   *30 minutes*
✦ Combine the vinegar, sugar and salt in a small, non-stick saucepan and boil until thick, about 5 minutes. Add the chili. Remove from the heat and cool.
✦ Soak the noodles in hot water until soft, about 2 to 3 minutes. Drain, then cut into ½ in (1 cm) pieces.
✦ Pour the chili mixture into a small serving bowl, add the cucumber and refrigerate.
✦ Combine the egg white and cold water in a bowl.

COOKING   *1 hour*
✦ Heat the sesame oil in a wok over medium heat. Add the chicken and garlic and cook, stirring continuously, for 5 minutes. Add the mushrooms, fish sauce, soy sauce and sugar. Cook, stirring, for 2 minutes.
✦ Remove from the heat, and stir in the noodles. Let stand until the liquid is absorbed, about 10 minutes
✦ Place a spring roll wrapper on a board with a corner facing you. Place 1 tablespoon of the filling about

one-third up from the corner. Fold the corner up and over the filling and fold in the sides. Brush the top corner with a little of the egg white mixture and roll up tightly to form a neat parcel. Press to seal the edges.
✦ Heat the vegetable oil in the wok over high heat to 375°F (190°C) and deep-fry, 3 or 4 rolls at a time, until golden, about 2 minutes. Using a slotted spoon, transfer to a plate lined with paper towels to drain, and keep warm. Continue assembling and deep-frying the spring rolls until all the wrappers and filling have been used.
✦ Serve the hot spring rolls with the cucumber dipping sauce.

PER SPRING ROLL
90 calories/ 375 kilojoules; 3 g protein; 2.9 g fat, 30% of calories (0.5 g saturated, 5.1% of calories; 0.9 g monounsaturated, 9.3%; 1.5 g polyunsaturated, 15.6%); 13 g carbohydrate; 0.5 g dietary fiber; 136 mg sodium; 0.3 mg iron; 4 mg cholesterol.

Deep-Fried Spring Rolls (left) and Chicken Satay

Braised Soy Sauce Chicken

CHIANG YU CHI

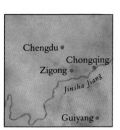

The sauce in which this chicken cools is known in China as a master sauce and can also be used with meat or fish. Stored in a covered jar, it will keep for two weeks in a refrigerator, indefinitely in a freezer.

SERVES 6

1 chicken, about 3 lb (1.5 kg)
1½ cups (12 fl oz/375 ml)
    reduced-sodium soy sauce
1½ cups (12 fl oz/375 ml) water
¼ cup (2 fl oz/60 ml) Chinese
    rice wine or pale dry sherry
½ teaspoon finely grated ginger
1 whole star anise
1 tablespoon sugar
½ teaspoon sesame oil
herbs, for garnish
mixed salad greens, for serving

PREPARATION   *10 minutes*
◆ Remove any visible fat from the chicken. Wash and pat dry thoroughly.

COOKING   *1 hour and 10 minutes*
plus 2 to 3 hours standing time
◆ Mix together the soy sauce, water, rice wine, ginger and star anise in a large saucepan. Bring to a boil. Add the chicken and cover the saucepan with a tight-fitting lid. Return to a boil, then reduce the heat and simmer for 30 minutes.
◆ Turn the chicken over. Stir in the sugar and baste the chicken with the cooking liquid. Cover and simmer, basting frequently, for an additional 25 minutes.
◆ Remove the saucepan from the heat and set aside, covered. Let the chicken cool in the liquid for 2 to 3 hours at room temperature.

◆ Transfer the chicken to a chopping board and brush lightly with the sesame oil. Cut the chicken into serving portions and arrange on a serving platter.
◆ Skim off any fat on the surface of the cooking liquid. Spoon 1 tablespoon of the cooking liquid over each portion and garnish with the herbs. Serve with the mixed salad greens.

PER SERVING
218 calories/913 kilojoules; 32 g protein; 5 g fat, 21% of calories (1.6 g saturated, 6.7% of calories; 2.4 g monounsaturated, 10.1%; 1 g polyunsaturated, 4.2%); 9 g carbohydrate; 0 g dietary fiber; 2148 mg sodium; 1.3 mg iron; 81 mg cholesterol.

Cold Chicken with Sesame and Spice Sauce

BAN BAN JI

This dish can be served either at room temperature or chilled. Chinese sesame paste is sold in Chinese grocery stores, but can be replaced by tahini (Middle Eastern sesame paste). The chili oil should be used sparingly; it keeps for long periods.

SERVES 6

SAUCE
4 garlic cloves, crushed
2 tablespoons Chinese sesame
    paste or tahini
1 tablespoon soy sauce
2 teaspoons chili oil
    (Chinese red oil)
2 teaspoons sugar
2 teaspoons white vinegar
1 teaspoon grated ginger
1 teaspoon salt
½ teaspoon ground Szechuan
    pepper (Chinese pepper)

1 tablespoon sesame oil
1½ lb (750 g) chicken breast
    fillets, thinly sliced
mixed salad greens, for serving

PREPARATION   *10 minutes*
◆ Combine the sauce ingredients in a small bowl.

COOKING   *10 minutes plus cooling time*
◆ Heat the oil in a large, non-stick skillet over medium heat. Add the chicken in small batches and cook until light golden, about 3 minutes per batch. As each batch is cooked, transfer it to a plate lined with paper towels. When all the chicken is cooked return it to the skillet.
◆ Remove the skillet from the heat and pour the sauce on top of the chicken. Cover the skillet and cool to room temperature.

◆ Transfer the chicken and sauce to a serving dish and serve with the mixed salad greens.

PER SERVING
236 calories/987 kilojoules; 30 g protein; 12 g fat, 47% of calories (2 g saturated, 8% of calories; 5.2 g monounsaturated, 20.2%; 4.8 g polyunsaturated, 18.8%); 2 g carbohydrate; 1 g dietary fiber; 557 mg sodium; 1.1 mg iron; 63 mg cholesterol.

Braised Soy Sauce Chicken

Chicken with Balsamic Vinegar
INSALATA DI CAPPONE ALL' ACETO BALSAMICO

SERVES 4

1 small green bell pepper
    (capsicum)
1 lb (500 g) chicken breast fillets
2 oz (60 g) drained, sundried
    tomatoes, packed in oil
1 small onion, cut into 8 wedges
1 bouquet garni
1 teaspoon black peppercorns
1 carrot, cut into julienne strips
1 stalk celery, cut into
    julienne strips
lettuce leaves, for serving

MARINADE

3 tablespoons balsamic vinegar
2 tablespoons dry white wine
2 tablespoons extra virgin
    olive oil

The best balsamic vinegar may be matured anywhere from 25 years to 75 years, or even longer. Authentic balsamics, in fact, are treated more like fine wines than vinegar. Balsamic vinegar is the perfect accompaniment to chicken.

PREPARATION   *20 minutes*
✦ Preheat the broiler (grill).
✦ Cut the bell pepper into 8 pieces and remove the core and seeds. Place the bell pepper pieces under the broiler, skin side up, and cook until tender and the skin has blistered. Cool and then rub off the skin.
✦ Cut the chicken fillets lengthwise into 1 in (2.5 cm) thick strips and slice the sundried tomatoes.
✦ Combine the marinade ingredients in a small bowl.

COOKING   *30 minutes plus 30 minutes standing time*
✦ Place the chicken in a large, heavy-bottomed sauce-pan with the onion, bouquet garni and peppercorns.
✦ Add boiling water just to cover and bring to a boil over low heat. Simmer until the chicken is cooked through, about 15 minutes. Using a slotted spoon, transfer the chicken to a serving platter and let cool for about 5 minutes. Discard the cooking liquid.
✦ Pour half the marinade over the chicken. Cover and refrigerate for 30 minutes, turning the chicken once.
✦ Arrange the chicken on a bed of lettuce. Place the carrot, celery, bell pepper and sundried tomatoes on top. Pour the remaining marinade on top and serve.

PER SERVING
266 calories/1113 kilojoules; 31 g protein; 10 g fat, 34% of calories (2.1 g saturated, 7% of calories; 6.7 g monounsaturated, 23%; 1.2 g polyunsaturated, 4%); 10 g carbohydrate; 1.3 g dietary fiber; 145 mg sodium; 1.1 mg iron; 63 mg cholesterol.

Warm Chicken Salad with Artichoke Hearts and Black Olives
INSALATA TIEPIDA DI POLLO CON CARCIOFI E OLIVE

SERVES 4

4 chicken breast fillets, about
    4 oz (125 g) each
1 tablespoon virgin olive oil
1 tablespoon lemon juice
1½ tablespoons coarsely
    chopped marjoram
1½ tablespoons coarsely
    chopped tarragon
1½ tablespoons coarsely
    chopped lemon thyme
¼ teaspoon salt
¼ cup (2 fl oz/60 ml) dry
    white wine
13 oz (410 g) canned artichoke
    hearts with their liquid
mixed green lettuce leaves
12 black olives

DRESSING

2 tablespoons extra virgin olive oil
1½ tablespoons lemon juice
2 teaspoons finely chopped tarragon

This dish from Florence has the fresh taste of lemon and herbs. It is ideal for a lunch or a light meal on a hot summer's evening. The heart of the artichoke is the base of the flower and has long been prized as a delicacy.

PREPARATION   *25 minutes*
✦ Preheat the oven to 350°F (180°C).
✦ Place the chicken fillets between 2 sheets of plastic wrap and flatten to an even thickness with a meat mallet.
✦ Combine the olive oil, lemon juice, herbs and salt in a small bowl. Spread one-quarter of the herb mixture over each chicken fillet. Starting at a narrow end, roll up tightly and secure with 2 toothpicks.
✦ Combine the dressing ingredients in a small bowl.

COOKING   *40 minutes*
✦ Place each piece of chicken on a piece of aluminum foil and fold up the edges. Pour 1 tablespoon of the wine over each piece and fold the foil into a parcel. Bake the chicken until cooked through, about 25 minutes. Cool in the foil for 10 minutes, then slice.

✦ Meanwhile, cut the artichokes into quarters. Place the artichokes and their liquid in a small saucepan and heat over low heat until warm through, about 2 to 3 minutes. Drain.
✦ Divide the lettuce leaves among 4 plates. Arrange the chicken, artichokes and olives on top and pour the dressing over.
✦ Serve with crusty Italian bread.

PER SERVING
290 calories/1214 kilojoules; 31 g protein; 15 g fat, 47% of calories (3 g saturated, 9.4% of calories; 10 g monounsaturated, 31.5%; 2 g polyunsaturated, 6.1%); 4 g carbohydrate; 4.2 g dietary fiber; 680 mg sodium; 1.8 mg iron; 62 mg cholesterol.

Warm Chicken Salad with
Artichoke Hearts and Black Olives

Cold Chicken with Walnut Sauce

SATSIVI

SERVES 6

1 cup (4 oz / 125 g) walnuts
2 garlic cloves
1 cup cilantro (coriander) leaves
1 tablespoon tarragon
1 small red chili
¼ teaspoon salt
1 cooked chicken, about
    3 lb (1.5 kg)
1 tablespoon virgin olive oil
1 large onion, sliced
2 teaspoons all-purpose
    (plain) flour
2¼ cups (18 fl oz / 560 ml)
    chicken stock, skimmed of fat
2 egg yolks
¼ teaspoon sweet paprika
¼ teaspoon ground fenugreek
¼ teaspoon ground coriander
¼ teaspoon ground turmeric
1 tablespoon white wine vinegar
mixed salad greens, for serving

The English translation of the Russian recipe title *Satsivi* is "eaten cold." This dish is best prepared in advance and refrigerated so the flavors have a chance to blend. Reduce the quantity of walnuts for a lower fat dish.

PREPARATION   *20 minutes*
◆ Place the walnuts, garlic, cilantro, tarragon, chili and salt in a food processor and process to a paste.
◆ Remove the skin from the chicken, take the meat off the bone and cut into bite-sized pieces.

COOKING   *15 minutes plus at least 8 hours chilling time*
◆ Heat the oil in a large, non-stick skillet over medium-high heat. Add the onion and cook until golden, about 5 minutes. Add the flour and cook, stirring continuously, for 2 minutes. Pour in the chicken stock, reduce the heat and simmer for 2 minutes. Stir in the walnut paste and cook for 1 minute.
◆ Add 1 tablespoon of the cooking liquid to the egg yolks in a small bowl and stir to combine. Then add to the skillet and stir in quickly. Add the sweet paprika,

fenugreek, coriander and turmeric and cook, stirring occasionally, for 5 minutes. Remove from the heat and stir in the vinegar.
◆ Combine the sauce with the chicken pieces in a large serving bowl. Cover and refrigerate for at least 8 hours, or overnight, before serving.
◆ Serve cold with mixed salad greens.

PER SERVING (MOST OF THE FAT COMES FROM THE WALNUTS)
*411 calories / 1720 kilojoules; 30 g protein; 31 g fat,
68% of calories (4.7 g saturated, 10.2% of calories;
9.6 g monounsaturated, 21%; 16.7 g polyunsaturated, 36.8%);
3 g carbohydrate; 2.5 g dietary fiber; 447 mg sodium; 2.2 mg iron;
161 mg cholesterol.*

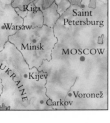

Shredded Chicken with Cilantro

SALAT IZ KURITSI S KINZOY

SERVES 4

½ cup (2 oz / 60 g) walnuts
1 lb (500 g) chicken breast fillets
1 tablespoon virgin olive oil
½ cup shallots (French shallots),
    sliced
1 teaspoon superfine (caster)
    sugar
lettuce leaves, for serving
cilantro (coriander) leaves,
    for garnish

DRESSING
½ cup cilantro (coriander) leaves,
    coarsely chopped
½ cup (4 oz / 125 g) light
    mayonnaise
¼ cup (2 oz / 60 g) light
    sour cream
1 teaspoon Dijon mustard
zest and juice of 1 lemon

Shallots combine beautifully with fresh cilantro in this easy-to-make Russian chicken salad. Serve with a salad of mixed greens and tomato. Reduce the quantity of walnuts for a lighter flavored, lower fat dish.

PREPARATION   *20 minutes*
◆ Toast the walnuts in a small, dry non-stick skillet over medium heat, stirring continuously, until golden, about 3 minutes.
◆ Combine the dressing ingredients in a bowl and mix thoroughly.

COOKING   *40 minutes*
◆ Place the chicken in a medium-sized saucepan, cover with cold water and bring to a boil. Cover, reduce the heat and simmer until tender, about 15 minutes. Remove from the heat, drain the chicken and slice thinly.
◆ Heat the oil in a small, non-stick skillet over low heat. Add the shallots and sugar and cook, stirring occasionally, until all the liquid has evaporated and the shallots are golden, about 20 minutes.

◆ Combine the chicken with the shallots and walnuts in a large bowl. Stir in the dressing and pile onto a serving platter with the lettuce leaves. Garnish with the cilantro leaves and serve immediately.

PER SERVING (MOST OF THE FAT COMES FROM THE WALNUTS)
437 calories / 1828 kilojoules; 33 g protein; 28 g fat, 57% of calories (4.6 g saturated, 9% of calories; 7.4 g monounsaturated, 15%; 16 g polyunsaturated, 33%); 13 g carbohydrate; 3.4 g dietary fiber; 447 mg sodium; 1.7 mg iron; 73 mg cholesterol.

Shredded Chicken with Cilantro

Spicy Ground Chicken

LAAB

SERVES 4

2 tablespoons (1 oz/30 g) short-grain rice

2 kaffir lime or lime leaves

3 tablespoons freshly squeezed lemon juice

3 tablespoons chicken stock, skimmed of fat

2 tablespoons fish sauce

1 small red chili, finely chopped

8 oz (250 g) ground (minced) chicken breast

3 shallots (French shallots) or 1 small red onion, finely chopped

1 small stalk lemongrass, thinly sliced

3 scallions (spring onions), chopped

4 crisp lettuce leaves

2 teaspoons chopped mint

½ teaspoon crushed dried chilies

A favorite of northern Thailand, this recipe is now enjoyed all over the country. Rice is dry-fried until golden brown and then ground to give texture to the dish—a reminder that rice is the basic grain in this area.

PREPARATION   *20 minutes*

◆ Toast the rice in a small, dry skillet, over low-medium heat, shaking constantly to prevent burning, until pale brown, about 4 to 5 minutes. Process in a blender until ground but not powdered.

◆ Use scissors to cut the kaffir lime leaves into thin slices.

COOKING   *15 minutes*

◆ Combine the lemon juice, chicken stock, fish sauce and red chili in a large, non-stick skillet or wok and bring to a boil. Add the chicken and cook, stirring and breaking up any lumps, until cooked through, about 6 to 8 minutes.

◆ Add the shallots, lemongrass, kaffir lime leaves, ground rice and scallions and cook for an additional

2 minutes. Remove from the heat and set aside to cool slightly, about 5 minutes.

◆ Line a serving dish with the lettuce leaves.

◆ Arrange the chicken mixture on the lettuce leaves, top with the chopped mint and sprinkle with the crushed chilies. Serve while still warm.

PER SERVING

120 calories/504 kilojoules; 16 g protein; 1 g fat, 12% of calories (0.4 g saturated, 4% of calories; 0.6 g monounsaturated, 7%; 0.1 g polyunsaturated, 1%); 10 g carbohydrate; 2 g dietary fiber; 626 mg sodium; 1 mg iron; 31 mg cholesterol.

Spicy Chicken and Papaya Salad

SOM TAM

SERVES 6

DRESSING

1½ tablespoons fish sauce

3 tablespoons freshly squeezed lime juice

¾ cup (6 fl oz/180 ml) coconut milk

1 small red chili, thinly sliced

2 tablespoons shredded cilantro (coriander) leaves

1 cooked chicken, about 3 lb (1.5 kg)

1 head romaine (cos) lettuce

1 green apple, sliced

1 banana, sliced and sprinkled with lime juice

½ papaya (pawpaw), peeled, seeded and sliced

4 shallots (French shallots), finely sliced

2 tablespoons roasted cashew nuts

parsley sprigs, for garnish

This colorful dish is quick and easy to make and the chicken is served chilled, so it can be prepared ahead. The smooth but spicy dressing is balanced by the cool, fresh fruit.

PREPARATION *20 minutes plus 1 hour refrigerating time*

◆ Combine the dressing ingredients well.

◆ Remove the skin from the chicken, take the meat off the bone and cut into bite-sized pieces. Place the chicken pieces in a large mixing bowl and pour the dressing on top. Combine well, cover and refrigerate for an hour.

◆ Separate the lettuce leaves, wash and dry.

ASSEMBLY   *5 minutes*

◆ Arrange the lettuce leaves in a large serving bowl and add the remaining salad ingredients. Place the chicken on top and pour over any dressing that is left in the mixing bowl.

◆ Sprinkle with the cashew nuts, garnish with the parsley sprigs and serve immediately.

PER SERVING

365 calories/1528 kilojoules; 39 g protein; 17 g fat, 42% of calories (8.9 g saturated, 22% of calories; 6 g monounsaturated, 15%; 2.1 g polyunsaturated, 5%); 14 g carbohydrate; 4.5 g dietary fiber; 204 mg sodium; 2.6 mg iron; 145 mg cholesterol.

Spicy Chicken and Papaya Salad

Chicken Salad

GOI GA

SERVES 6

1 small cucumber
1 teaspoon salt
4 gherkins, thinly sliced, plus
    3 tablespoons of their liquid
2 tablespoons apple cider vinegar
½ teaspoon crushed garlic
1 teaspoon sugar
1 onion, sliced
2 small red chilies, seeded
1 cooked chicken, about
    3 lb (1.5 kg)
2 carrots, cut into julienne strips
1 head romaine (cos) lettuce
¼ cup shredded cilantro
    (coriander) leaves
½ cup (2 oz/60 g) crushed
    peanuts

Marinating the onion in vinegar is essential to the success of this dish, as it partially pickles the onion and prevents its flavor from overpowering the other elements of this fresh-tasting salad.

PREPARATION   *30 minutes*

◆ Slice the cucumber, place in a bowl and sprinkle with the salt. Let stand for 15 minutes. Drain and pat dry with a paper towel to remove excess salt.
◆ Combine the gherkin liquid, vinegar, garlic and sugar in a small serving bowl. Add the onion, chilies and gherkins and mix well. Let stand for 15 minutes.
◆ Separate the lettuce leaves, wash and dry.
◆ Remove the skin from the chicken, take the meat off the bone and cut into bite-sized pieces.

ASSEMBLY   *10 minutes*

◆ Place the chicken in a large bowl, add the cucumber and carrots. Moisten with 1 tablespoon of the onion and chili dressing and toss well. Arrange the salad on a bed of the lettuce leaves on a serving platter. Sprinkle the cilantro and peanuts on top.
◆ Serve with the bowl of dressing.

PER SERVING
233 calories/976 kilojoules; 27 g protein; 10 g fat, 40% of calories (2.8 g saturated, 11% of calories; 4.9 g monounsaturated, 20%; 2.3 g polyunsaturated, 9%); 8 g carbohydrate; 3.1 g dietary fiber; 477 mg sodium; 1.5 mg iron; 102 mg cholesterol.

Chicken and Cabbage Salad

GA XE PHAI

SERVES 6

½ cup (4 fl oz/125 ml) white
    wine vinegar
1 tablespoon sugar
½ teaspoon salt
1 small onion, finely sliced
1 cooked chicken, about
    3 lb (1.5 kg)
¼ head cabbage, finely shredded
1 carrot, grated
½ cup chopped Vietnamese mint
½ teaspoon fish sauce
Vietnamese mint leaves, for
    garnish

Vietnamese mint, with its distinctive hot flavor, is used extensively in cooking. Known as *rau ram,* it has long, dark green leaves and is available from specialty Asian food stores. If necessary, a combination of mint and coriander can be used instead.

PREPARATION   *15 minutes plus marinating time*

◆ Combine the vinegar, sugar and salt in a bowl. Add the onion and marinate for 30 minutes.
◆ Remove the skin from the chicken, take the meat off the bone and cut into bite-sized pieces.

ASSEMBLY   *10 minutes*

◆ Place the chicken, cabbage, carrot, chopped mint, fish sauce and the onion mixture in a large serving bowl and toss well.
◆ Serve, garnished with the mint leaves.

PER SERVING
204 calories/855 kilojoules; 20 g protein; 11 g fat, 50% of calories (3.7 g saturated, 17% of calories; 5.5 g monounsaturated, 25%; 1.8 g polyunsaturated, 8%); 5 g carbohydrate; 2.2 g dietary fiber; 243 mg sodium; 1.6 mg iron; 84 mg cholesterol.

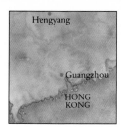

Hengyang

Guangzhou

HONG KONG

Chicken with Orange Zest and Red Chili

JU ZI PI JI

SERVES 6

MARINADE

1 teaspoon chopped orange zest
1 tablespoon Chinese rice wine
4 teaspoons soy sauce
1 teaspoon grated ginger
2 tablespoons freshly squeezed
  orange juice

1½ lb (750 g) chicken breast
  fillets, thinly sliced
1 tablespoon vegetable oil
1 onion, cut into 12 wedges
1 teaspoon dried, crushed red
  chilies
4 scallions (spring onions), sliced

SAUCE

¼ cup (2 fl oz/60 ml) freshly
  squeezed orange juice
2 teaspoons sugar
1 tablespoon soy sauce
1 teaspoon vinegar
1 teaspoon sesame oil
1 teaspoon cornstarch (cornflour)

This fresh-tasting Chinese dish makes a good lunchtime choice. It is cooked quickly in the wok, ensuring that the traditional flavors of sweet (sugar), sour (vinegar) and hot (chili) are distributed and absorbed throughout.

PREPARATION   *20 minutes plus*
                           20 minutes marinating time

✦ Toast the orange zest in a small, dry, non-stick skillet over medium-high heat, stirring continuously until the pieces turn brown, about 2 to 3 minutes.
✦ Combine the remaining marinade ingredients with the orange zest in a small mixing bowl. Pour the marinade over the chicken, cover and leave to marinate in the refrigerator for 20 minutes.
✦ Combine the sauce ingredients in a small mixing bowl.

COOKING   *20 minutes*

✦ Remove the chicken pieces from the marinade with a slotted spoon and reserve the marinade.
✦ Heat 2 teaspoons of the oil in a wok over medium-high heat and add the chicken in small batches. Stir-fry each batch until golden, about 5 minutes per batch. Using a slotted spoon, transfer to a plate and set aside.

✦ Add the remaining oil and the marinade to the wok and heat gently. Add the onion and the crushed chilies and cook until the onion is soft, about 3 minutes.
✦ Return the chicken to the wok, add the scallions and cook for 1 minute. Add the prepared sauce and cook, stirring, over medium heat until the mixture has thickened, about 1 minute. Place the chicken in a deep serving dish, spoon the sauce on top and serve with boiled rice.

PER SERVING
192 calories/804 kilojoules; 29 g protein; 6.1 g fat, 28% of calories (1.3 g saturated, 16% of calories; 2.6 g monounsaturated, 12%; 2.2 g polyunsaturated, 10%); 4 g carbohydrate; 0.5 g dietary fiber; 442 mg sodium; 1 mg iron; 63 mg cholesterol.

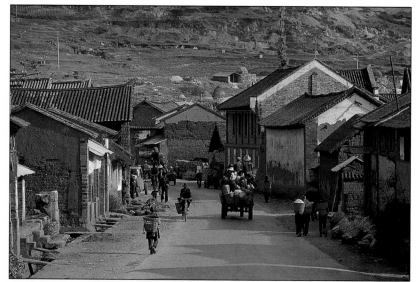

Most people still get around on foot or by bicycle in rural China; motor vehicles are a relatively rare sight.

Chicken with Orange Zest and Red Chili

Chengtu Chicken
CHENH-DU JI

SERVES 6

1½ tablespoons Chinese rice wine
1 tablespoon soy sauce
1½ lb (750 g) chicken breast
    fillets, thinly sliced
5 teaspoons vegetable oil
1 teaspoon grated ginger
2 garlic cloves, crushed
1 tablespoon chili paste (Chinese
    hot bean paste)
½ teaspoon Szechuan pepper
    (Chinese pepper)
2 vine-ripened tomatoes, diced
4 shallots (French shallots), sliced
2 cups (4 oz / 125 g) bean sprouts

SAUCE

2 teaspoons cornstarch (cornflour)
3 teaspoons soy sauce
1 teaspoon white vinegar
1 teaspoon sugar
2 teaspoons sesame oil
1 teaspoon Chinese sesame paste

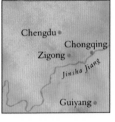

Chengtu is the capital of the province of Szechuan. Szechuan cooking is known for its distinctive, highly seasoned flavor. Szechuan pepper is unique to this area and has an unmistakable sour-peppery aftertaste.

PREPARATION   *15 minutes plus*
                          10 minutes marinating time
◆ Combine the rice wine and soy sauce in a large mixing bowl. Add the chicken and leave to marinate for 10 minutes.
◆ Combine the sauce ingredients in a small bowl.

COOKING   *20 minutes*
◆ Heat 3 teaspoons of the oil in a wok over medium-high heat. Add the chicken and stir-fry in small batches until golden, about 5 minutes per batch. Using a slotted spoon, remove the chicken and set aside.
◆ Add the remaining oil to the wok, then add the ginger, garlic, chili paste and Szechuan pepper. Cook, stirring continuously, for 1 minute.

◆ Return the chicken to the wok, add the tomatoes and shallots and stir-fry for 1 minute.
◆ Stir in the prepared sauce and cook for an additional minute, then stir in the bean sprouts. Cook for an additional minute.
◆ Place on a serving platter and serve immediately with boiled rice.

PER SERVING
218 calories / 913 kilojoules; 30 g protein; 8.7 g fat, 35% of calories (1.7 g saturated, 7% of calories; 3.4 g monounsaturated, 13.7%; 3.6 g polyunsaturated, 14.3%); 4 g carbohydrate; 1.8 g dietary fiber; 404 mg sodium; 1.3 mg iron; 63 mg cholesterol.

Sliced Chicken and Vegetables
SU JIAO JI PIAN

SERVES 4

1 lb (500 g) chicken breast fillets
2 tablespoons vegetable oil
1 teaspoon hot chili sauce
2 garlic cloves, crushed
1 teaspoon grated ginger
6 scallions (spring onions), sliced
5 oz (155 g) zucchini (courgettes),
    cut into julienne strips
2 teaspoons soy sauce
2 teaspoons Chinese rice wine
¼ teaspoon Szechuan pepper
    (Chinese pepper)
2 teaspoons white vinegar
2 teaspoons sugar
½ cup (4 fl oz / 125 ml) chicken
    stock, skimmed of fat
2 teaspoons cornstarch (cornflour)
herbs, for garnish

Because chicken doesn't have a strong flavor of its own, it is the perfect base for the complex layers of flavors that typify Szechuan cooking. This dish is a good example of home-style cooking from this western province.

PREPARATION   *15 minutes*
◆ Cut the chicken fillets into thin slices for stir-frying.

COOKING   *20 minutes*
◆ Heat the oil in a wok over medium-high heat. Add the chicken in small batches and stir-fry until cooked, about 5 minutes per batch. Using a slotted spoon, remove the chicken and set aside.
◆ Add the chili sauce, garlic, ginger, scallions and zucchini to the wok and cook over medium heat, stirring continuously, for 2 minutes. Add the soy sauce, rice wine, Szechuan pepper and vinegar and cook for 1 minute. Return the chicken to the wok with the

sugar and continue cooking for an additional minute.
◆ Combine the stock and cornstarch in a small bowl, then add to the wok, stirring. Reduce the heat and simmer until thickened, about 1 minute.
◆ Place in a deep serving dish and spoon the sauce on top. Garnish with the herbs and serve with boiled rice.

PER SERVING
232 calories / 969 kilojoules; 29 g protein; 10 g fat, 39% of calories (1.8 g saturated, 7% of calories; 4.4 g monounsaturated, 17%; 3.8 g polyunsaturated, 15%); 5 g carbohydrate; 1.4 g dietary fiber; 267 mg sodium; 1.2 mg iron; 63 mg cholesterol.

Sliced Chicken and Vegetables

Chengdu
Chongqing
Zigong
Jinsha Jiang
Guiyang

Peppery and Hot Chicken

MA LA ZI JI

This spicy, peppery dish comes from the province of Szechuan in western China. Szechuan pepper (also known as *fagara*) has a distinct flavor for which there is no substitute. Shop for it, as well as for Chinese hot bean paste, in Asian food stores.

SERVES 6

MARINADE

1 tablespoon cornstarch (cornflour)
1 tablespoon Chinese rice wine
1 egg white

1½ lb (750 g) chicken breast fillets, thinly sliced
5 teaspoons vegetable oil
4 scallions (spring onions), chopped
2 teaspoons grated ginger
3 garlic cloves, crushed
1 tablespoon chili paste (Chinese hot bean paste)

SAUCE

2 teaspoons cornstarch (cornflour)
1 chicken bouillon (stock) cube
1 tablespoon soy sauce
1 tablespoon water
2 teaspoons vinegar
2 teaspoons sesame oil
1 teaspoon ground Szechuan pepper (Chinese pepper)

PREPARATION   *15 minutes*
plus 20 minutes marinating time

◆ To make the marinade, combine the cornstarch with the wine in a small bowl and then beat in the egg white. Pour on top of the chicken, cover and leave to marinate in the refrigerator for 20 minutes.

COOKING   *20 minutes*

◆ Heat 3 teaspoons of the oil in a large, non-stick skillet over medium-high heat. Add the chicken and stir-fry in batches for about 5 minutes per batch. Using a slotted spoon, remove the chicken and set aside.
◆ Heat the remaining oil in the skillet, then add the scallions, ginger and garlic and cook for 1 minute. Return the chicken to the skillet and add the chili paste. Cook for an additional minute.

◆ Combine the cornstarch, bouillon cube, soy sauce, water, vinegar, sesame oil and Szechuan pepper in a bowl. Pour into the skillet, reduce the heat to medium and cook until the mixture has thickened, about 1 minute.
◆ Place in a deep serving dish and spoon the sauce on top. Serve with boiled rice.

PER SERVING
214 calories/895 kilojoules; 29 g protein; 8.8 g fat, 40% of calories (1.8 g saturated, 8% of calories; 3.4 g monounsaturated, 15.6%; 3.6 g polyunsaturated, 16.4%); 4 g carbohydrate; 0.5 g dietary fiber; 399 mg sodium; 1 mg iron; 63 mg cholesterol.

Tending the rice in a paddy field near Jinghong in southern China.

Chicken with Cider

COQ AU CIDRE

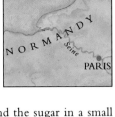

Normandy, a dairy-farming area of France, boasts the richest cream of the country. Apples also grow in abundance in this area and many are made into cider. This dish combines these two ingredients synonymous with Normandy.

SERVES 6

⅓ cup (1½ oz / 45 g) all-purpose
    (plain) flour
1 teaspoon salt
1 tablespoon paprika
12 boneless, skinless chicken
    thighs (thigh fillets), about
    2 oz (60 g) each
2 green eating apples
4 teaspoons butter
1 tablespoon vegetable oil
1 onion, finely diced
1¾ cups (14 fl oz / 440 ml) hard
    (dry) cider
1 tablespoon heavy (thick) cream
1 teaspoon superfine (caster) sugar
6 shallots (French shallots),
    finely sliced
2 carrots, about 7 oz (220 g),
    cut into julienne strips
1 stalk celery, cut into 6 pieces
1 bouquet garni
herbs, for garnish

PREPARATION   *20 minutes*

✦ Preheat the oven to 350°F (180°C).
✦ Combine 4 tablespoons of the flour with the salt and paprika in a clean, plastic bag. Add the chicken and coat with the seasoned flour. Shake off the excess flour.
✦ Core but do not peel the apples, then cut each apple into 8 wedges.

COOKING   *1¼ hours*

✦ Heat half of the butter and all of the oil in a medium-sized, non-stick skillet over medium-high heat. Add the chicken in 2 batches and cook until brown, about 5 minutes per batch. Using a slotted spoon, remove the chicken and set aside.
✦ Add the onion to the skillet and cook until soft, about 3 minutes. Stir in the remaining flour and gradually mix in the cider. Cook until thickened, about 1 minute. Stir in the cream and remove from the heat.

✦ Place the remaining butter and the sugar in a small saucepan over medium heat. After the butter melts, add the shallots, carrots and celery and cook, stirring, to caramelize the vegetables, about 10 minutes.
✦ Arrange the vegetables and the apple segments on the bottom and around the sides of a large casserole dish and add the bouquet garni and the chicken. Pour the cider sauce on top, cover and bake until cooked through, about 40 minutes. Remove the bouquet garni, then serve, sprinkled with the herbs.

PER SERVING
310 calories / 1298 kilojoules; 25 g protein; 14 g fat,
39% of calories (6.5 g saturated, 17.9% of calories;
5.7 g monounsaturated, 16%; 1.8 g polyunsaturated, 5.1%);
20 g carbohydrate; 3 g dietary fiber; 461 mg sodium; 0.8 mg iron;
172 mg cholesterol.

Windowboxes of bright geraniums are typical of buildings in the picturesque town of Montrèsor.

Chicken with Mushrooms
POULET AUX CHAMPIGNONS A LA MODE DE NORMANDIE

Hunting for mushrooms in the woods is one of the pleasures of trips into the country for many French families. Mushrooms are used in many French recipes in both the simplest and most exotic dishes.

SERVES 6

1 chicken, about 3 lb (1.5 kg)
1 tablespoon virgin olive oil
¼ teaspoon freshly ground black pepper
8 oz (250 g) button mushrooms, sliced
juice of ½ lemon
1 onion, finely chopped
3 garlic cloves, crushed
1 tablespoon tarragon sprigs
1 tablespoon parsley sprigs
1 tablespoon thyme sprigs
¾ cup (6 fl oz/180 ml) hard (dry) cider
½ cup (4 fl oz/125 ml) chicken stock, skimmed of fat
½ teaspoon salt
¼ teaspoon cayenne pepper
1 teaspoon cornstarch (cornflour)
2 tablespoons light sour cream

PREPARATION   *10 minutes*
◆ Preheat the oven to 350°F (180°C).
◆ Split the chicken down the backbone. Press down firmly with the palm of your hand to flatten. Brush the chicken with 1 teaspoon of the oil and sprinkle with the black pepper.
◆ Soak the mushrooms in the lemon juice and set aside.

COOKING   *1 hour*
◆ Heat the remaining oil in a large, flameproof casserole dish over medium-high heat. Add the onion and garlic and cook until the onion is soft, about 3 minutes. Place the chicken on top.
◆ Combine the herbs, cider, chicken stock, salt and cayenne pepper in a bowl, then pour on top of the chicken. Cover and bake until the juices run clear when the chicken is tested with a skewer, about 45 minutes.

◆ Transfer the chicken to a plate and keep warm.
◆ Add the mushrooms to the casserole dish. In a small bowl, combine the cornstarch with 1 tablespoon of the cooking liquid, then stir into the mushroom mixture. Cook over medium heat, stirring occasionally, until the sauce has thickened and the mushrooms are soft, about 5 minutes. Remove the casserole dish from the heat and stir in the sour cream.
◆ Cut the chicken into serving portions, place on a warm serving platter and pour the sauce on top. Serve with fresh steamed vegetables.

PER SERVING
276 calories/1156 kilojoules; 27 g protein; 16 g fat, 54% of calories (5.3 g saturated, 18 % of calories; 8.3 g monounsaturated, 28%; 2.4 g polyunsaturated, 8%); 3 g carbohydrate; 1.8 g dietary fiber; 235 mg sodium; 1.4 mg iron; 87 mg cholesterol.

Chicken with Artichokes
POULET A LA MONSELET

Artichokes are a member of the thistle family. They were introduced to France by Catherine de Medici in 1533, and became so popular they are now grown in large quantities in northern France.

SERVES 4

3 tablespoons all-purpose (plain) flour
1 teaspoon salt
pinch freshly ground black pepper
8 boneless, skinless chicken thighs (thigh fillets), about 2 oz (60 g) each
2 large potatoes, thinly sliced
2 cups (12 oz/375 g) canned artichoke hearts, drained
2 tablespoons vegetable oil
4 small onions, halved lengthwise
¾ cup (6 fl oz/180 ml) dry white wine
¾ cup (6 fl oz/180 ml) chicken stock, skimmed of fat
1 teaspoon chopped thyme, plus extra for garnish
2 small bay leaves
1 tablespoon chopped parsley

PREPARATION   *15 minutes*
◆ Preheat the oven to 350°F (180°C).
◆ Combine the flour, salt and pepper in a clean, plastic bag. Add the chicken and coat with the seasoned flour. Shake off the excess flour.
◆ Parcook the potatoes in the microwave for 5 minutes, or steam for 7 minutes. Do not overcook—they should still be crunchy.
◆ Halve the artichokes,

COOKING   *1 hour*
◆ Heat the oil in a medium-sized, non-stick skillet over medium-high heat. Add the chicken in 2 batches and cook until brown, about 5 minutes per batch. Using a slotted spoon, remove the chicken and set aside.
◆ Reduce the heat to medium, add the onions and

cook until golden brown, about 5 minutes.
◆ Place the potatoes, onions and artichoke hearts in a casserole dish. Add the chicken. Combine the wine, chicken stock, thyme, bay leaves and parsley in a bowl, then pour on top of the chicken.
◆ Bake, covered, until the chicken is cooked through, about 40 minutes. Serve, garnished with the extra chopped thyme.

PER SERVING
357 calories/1494 kilojoules; 28 g protein; 15 g fat, 38% of calories (3.5 g saturated, 8.7% of calories; 7.1 g monounsaturated, 17.9%; 4.4 g polyunsaturated, 11.4%); 21 g carbohydrate; 5.5 g dietary fiber; 942 mg sodium; 1.4 mg iron; 162 mg cholesterol.

Chicken with Artichokes

Roast Chicken with Pine Nuts

POULET AUX PIGNONS

1 chicken, about 3 lb (1.5 kg)
zest and juice of 1 lemon
1½ tablespoons chopped tarragon
1½ tablespoons chopped basil
1 tablespoon chopped thyme
½ cup (4 fl oz/125 ml) dry
    white wine
2 teaspoons virgin olive oil
¼ teaspoon salt
¼ teaspoon freshly ground black
    pepper
¼ cup (1 oz/30 g) pine nuts
mixed salad leaves, for serving
edible flowers, for garnish

This dish comes from Provence, where herbs grow in profusion and play a key role in cooking. Here thyme, tarragon and basil are used. If fresh herbs are unavailable, dry herbs may be substituted; simply divide the quantities by four.

PREPARATION   *15 minutes*

✦ Preheat the oven to 400°F (200°C).
✦ Split the chicken down the backbone. Press down firmly with the palm of your hand to flatten. Separate the skin from the flesh, beginning at the tail end of the chicken. Mix the lemon zest and herbs together and spread over the flesh. Replace the skin and secure with a toothpick.

COOKING   *1 hour*

✦ Place the chicken, cavity side up, on a rack in a roasting pan. Combine the lemon juice with the white wine in a small bowl, then pour on top of the chicken. Roast for 15 minutes.

✦ Turn the chicken over, baste with the pan juices and brush with the oil. Sprinkle with the salt and pepper. Roast until the skin is crisp and golden and the juices run clear when the chicken is tested with a skewer, about 40 minutes.
✦ Meanwhile, toast the pine nuts in a small, dry skillet over medium heat until golden, about 1 minute.
✦ Cut the chicken into serving pieces, and place on a bed of the salad leaves. Sprinkle the pine nuts and flowers on top and serve.

PER SERVING

299 calories/1251 kilojoules; 26 g protein; 20 g fat, 59% of calories (5.1 g saturated, 15% of calories; 9.4 g monounsaturated, 28%; 5.5 g polyunsaturated, 16%); 1 g carbohydrate; 1.4 g dietary fiber; 159 mg sodium; 1.5 mg iron; 83 mg cholesterol.

Café patrons enjoy the afternoon sun on Boulevard St Germain in Paris.

Roast Chicken with Pine Nuts

Chicken in Red Wine

COQ AU VIN

SERVES 6

1 chicken, about 3 lb (1.5 kg)
1 tablespoon virgin olive oil
1 tablespoon butter
4 oz (125 g) lean bacon, chopped
12 small shallots (French shallots)
1 large onion, chopped
1 carrot, sliced
1 garlic clove, finely chopped
1 tablespoon brandy
2 tablespoons all-purpose (plain)
    flour
1 tablespoon chopped marjoram
½ teaspoon chopped thyme
1 bay leaf
1 teaspoon salt
¼ teaspoon freshly ground black
    pepper
2 cups (16 fl oz/500 ml) dry
    red wine
2 cups (8 oz/250 g) button
    mushrooms
herb sprigs, for garnish

Originally devised for serving up a tough, old farmyard cock, this traditional recipe is now regarded as a classic of French cuisine, demanding ingredients of the best quality. If morels are available, use them instead of button mushrooms.

PREPARATION   *15 minutes*
✦ Cut the chicken into serving pieces and remove any visible fat.

COOKING   *1½ hours*
✦ Heat the oil and butter in a large, heavy-bottomed saucepan over medium-high heat. Add the bacon and cook, stirring occasionally, for 3 minutes. Push to one side of the saucepan, add the shallots, onion, carrot and garlic and cook until the onion is soft, about 3 minutes. Using a slotted spoon, remove the vegetables and set aside.
✦ Add the chicken to the saucepan and cook until well browned on both sides, about 5 minutes per side.
✦ Heat the brandy in a small saucepan over low heat for 1 minute. Carefully ignite with a taper and pour over the chicken.
✦ Add the flour, marjoram, thyme, bay leaf, salt and

pepper to the saucepan and stir to combine. Gradually add the red wine, stirring continuously. Return the vegetables to the saucepan, cover, reduce the heat and simmer until the chicken is tender, about 1 hour. During the last 10 minutes of cooking, add the mushrooms, stirring to mix thoroughly.
✦ Skim off any excess fat from the sauce. Discard the bay leaf and adjust the seasoning, if necessary.
✦ Arrange the chicken pieces on a warm serving dish, spoon the sauce and vegetables on top. Garnish with the herb sprigs and serve.

PER SERVING
376 calories/1572 kilojoules; 32 g protein; 19 g fat, 46% of calories (5.7 g saturated, 14% of calories; 10.5 g monounsaturated, 25%; 2.8 g polyunsaturated, 7%); 5 g carbohydrate; 2.1 g dietary fiber; 741 mg sodium; 1.8 mg iron; 95 mg cholesterol.

Chicken Stuffed with Basil

POULET FARCI AU BASILIC

SERVES 4

½ cup basil leaves, plus extra
    for garnish
2 tablespoons virgin olive oil
4 chicken breast fillets, about
    4 oz (125 g) each
1 leek, thinly sliced
3 tablespoons light cream
salt, to taste
freshly ground black pepper,
    to taste

Spirituelle, or witty, is how the Provençaux describe their cuisine, which is more reminiscent of Mediterranean cooking than it is of the cooking of other regions of France. In this recipe, a basil purée is used to flavor chicken fillets.

PREPARATION   *10 minutes*
✦ Chop the basil leaves finely, or pound them to a purée in a mortar. Mix well with 4 teaspoons of the oil and set aside.

COOKING   *30 minutes*
✦ Place the chicken fillets between 2 sheets of plastic wrap and flatten to an even thickness with a meat mallet. Place 2 teaspoons of the basil purée on each fillet and roll up. Secure with toothpicks.
✦ Brush the chicken rolls with 1 teaspoon of the oil. Place the rolls in a large, non-stick skillet and cook over moderate heat, or broil (grill), turning frequently, until cooked through and tender, about 20 minutes.
✦ Meanwhile, heat the remaining oil in a small sauce-

pan over low heat. Add the leek and cook, stirring occasionally, for about 5 minutes. Add the cream and the remaining basil purée. Season with the salt and pepper and cook until heated through, about 2 minutes.
✦ Divide the basil and leek mixture among 4 plates. Place a chicken roll on each plate. Garnish with the extra basil and serve.

PER SERVING
238 calories/997 kilojoules; 29 g protein; 13 g fat, 50% of calories (3.7 g saturated, 14% of calories; 7.7 g monounsaturated, 30%; 1.6 g polyunsaturated, 6%); 2 g carbohydrate; 0.8 g dietary fiber; 177 mg sodium; 1.1 mg iron; 70 mg cholesterol.

Chicken in Red Wine

Chicken in White Wine

POULET AU VIN BLANC

SERVES 4

*4 chicken breasts, about 8 oz
   (250 g) each*
1 tablespoon vegetable oil
1 onion, finely chopped
3 garlic cloves, crushed
1 teaspoon margarine
2 carrots, sliced
*2 tablespoons Calvados or other
   apple brandy*
*⅓ cup (3 fl oz/90 ml) dry white
   wine*
¼ teaspoon ground nutmeg
½ teaspoon salt
*¼ teaspoon freshly ground black
   pepper*
1 bouquet garni
1 egg yolk
2 tablespoons light sour cream
chopped parsley, for garnish

Cream, eggs, butter, cheese and cider form the true foundation of the cooking of Normandy. Here, Calvados, the region's world-renowned apple brandy, is used to set aflame a skillet of chicken breasts before they are placed in a casserole dish and baked.

PREPARATION   *10 minutes*
✦ Preheat the oven to 350°F (180°C).
✦ Remove the skin from the chicken.

COOKING   *1 hour and 20 minutes*
✦ Melt 2 teaspoons of the oil in a large, non-stick skillet over medium-high heat. Add the chicken in 2 batches, cooking until just browned on each side, about 5 minutes per batch. Using a slotted spoon, transfer to a plate.
✦ Add the remaining oil and the onion and garlic and cook until the onion is soft, about 3 minutes. Using a slotted spoon, transfer to the plate with the chicken.
✦ Add the margarine to the same skillet and melt over low heat for 1 minute. Add the carrots and increase the heat to medium-high. Cook, stirring continuously, for 2 minutes. Return the chicken, onion and garlic to the skillet and cook until heated through, about 3 minutes.
✦ Heat the Calvados for 20 seconds on High in a microwave oven, or heat in a small saucepan over medium heat for 1 minute. Pour on top of the chicken and set aflame carefully with a taper. When the flames die down, place the chicken mixture in a flameproof casserole dish.
✦ Combine the wine, nutmeg, salt and pepper in a small bowl, then pour into the casserole dish. Add the bouquet garni. Bake, covered, until the juices run clear when the chicken is tested with a skewer, about 45 minutes. Transfer the chicken to a plate and keep warm. Remove the bouquet garni from the casserole dish and discard.
✦ Mix together the egg yolk, sour cream and 2 tablespoons of liquid from the casserole.
✦ Place the casserole dish on top of the stove over medium heat and bring the cooking juices to a boil, then remove from the heat and stir in the egg mixture. Return the chicken to the casserole dish, garnish with the chopped parsley and serve.

PER SERVING
259 calories/1086 kilojoules; 30 g protein; 10 g fat, 35% of calories (3 g saturated, 10.5% of calories; 4.2 g monounsaturated, 14.7%; 2.8 g polyunsaturated, 9.8%); 4 g carbohydrate; 2.1 g dietary fiber; 356 mg sodium; 1.2 mg iron; 112 mg cholesterol.

*Specialty food
stores of all kinds
bring the best
regional specialties
to Parisian shoppers.*

Goan Curry

SHAKOOTHI

1 in (2.5 cm) ginger
¼ whole nutmeg
⅓ cup shredded coconut plus
    extra for garnish
4 cloves
1 in (2.5 cm) cinnamon stick
1 teaspoon ground coriander
1 teaspoon ground turmeric
½ teaspoon cardamom seeds
½ teaspoon whole black
    peppercorns
2 tablespoons vegetable oil
5 garlic cloves, finely chopped
2 small red chilies, finely
    chopped
¾ cup (6 fl oz / 180 ml) water
1 large onion, finely chopped
8 skinless chicken drumsticks,
    about 4 oz (125 g) each
1 teaspoon salt

In this distinctive dish from the west coast of India, the coconut is first dry roasted and then blended with spices. Many Goan recipes toast the spices to strengthen the flavors.

PREPARATION   *10 minutes*
◆ Peel and grate the ginger.
◆ Finely grate the nutmeg.

COOKING   *50 minutes*
◆ Toast the coconut in a large, dry, non-stick skillet, stirring continuously, over medium heat, for about 1 minute. Add the nutmeg, cloves, cinnamon, coriander, turmeric, cardamom and peppercorns and toast, stirring continuously, for 2 minutes. Place the mixture in a blender and process until finely ground. Transfer to a bowl.
◆ Heat 1 tablespoon of the oil in the skillet over medium heat. Add the garlic, ginger and chilies and cook for 2 minutes. Place in the blender, add ¼ cup of the water and purée.
◆ Add the remaining oil to the skillet and heat gently.

Add the onion and cook until soft and golden, about 3 minutes. Stir in the chili mixture.
◆ Add the chicken, salt and spice mix to the skillet. Cook over medium heat, stirring to coat the chicken, for 5 minutes. Add the remaining water and bring to a boil. Reduce the heat, cover and simmer until the juices run clear when the chicken is tested with a skewer, about 30 minutes. Turn the chicken frequently during cooking.
◆ Place the chicken on a serving dish, spoon the sauce on top and serve with rice.

PER SERVING
*278 calories/1162 kilojoules; 25 g protein; 19 g fat,
59% of calories (7.6 g saturated, 23.6% of calories;
6.1 g monounsaturated, 18.9%; 5.3 g polyunsaturated, 16.5%);
3 g carbohydrate; 2.4 g dietary fiber; 597 mg sodium; 2.2 mg iron;
103 mg cholesterol.*

People washing in the sacred Ganges River at Yaranasi; the Ganges is believed to have the power to cleanse sins.

Marinated Spiced Chicken

TANDOORI MURGH

Tandoori is India's version of barbecued chicken. The chicken is tenderized and flavored in a yogurt marinade, seasoned with ginger and garlic and traditionally cooked in a clay oven heated with charcoal or wood.

SERVES 4

1 teaspoon hot chili powder
1 tablespoon lemon juice
4 chicken breast fillets, about
   4 oz (125 g) each

MARINADE

2 tablespoons plain yogurt
2 garlic cloves
1 tablespoon raisins
1 in (2.5 cm) ginger
½ teaspoon cumin seeds
2 teaspoons ground coriander
1 small red chili

PREPARATION   *20 minutes plus 3 hours marinating time*
✦ Combine the chili powder and the lemon juice.
✦ Make several cuts in the chicken. Brush the lemon mixture over the chicken and set aside for 20 minutes.
✦ Place the marinade ingredients in a blender and purée. Pour on top of the chicken, cover and marinate in the refrigerator for 3 hours.
✦ Preheat the oven to 400°F (200°C).

COOKING   *45 minutes*
✦ Add water just to cover the base of a roasting pan; this will prevent burning. Place the chicken on a rack in the pan, reserving the marinade in the refrigerator. Roast the chicken, basting frequently with the marinade, until tender, about 40 minutes.
✦ Place the chicken on a serving platter and serve immediately.

PER SERVING

157 calories/657 kilojoules; 29 g protein; 3.3 g fat, 19% of calories (1.2 g saturated, 7% of calories; 1.6 g monounsaturated, 9%; 0.5 g polyunsaturated, 3%); 3 g carbohydrate; 0.5 g dietary fiber; 76 mg sodium; 0.9 mg iron; 64 mg cholesterol.

Chicken with Cardamom

MURGH ILAYDRI

Spices are the essence of Indian cooking. *Masala* refers to any blend of spices and can be either dry or wet. Wet *masalas* are typical of southern India, whereas dry *masalas* (with dried spices ground and combined), come from the north.

SERVES 4

MASALA

¾ cup (6½ oz/200 g) plain
   yogurt
½ teaspoon cardamom seeds
½ in (2 cm) ginger
2 garlic cloves
½ teaspoon fennel seeds
¼ teaspoon cayenne pepper

1 lb (500 g) chicken breast fillets
3 tablespoons (1½ oz/45 g)
   ghee or butter
generous pinch saffron threads
1 tablespoon boiling water
1 in (2.5 cm) cinnamon stick
1 clove
2 onions, chopped
3 tablespoons water

PREPARATION   *15 minutes plus 1 hour marinating time*
✦ Place the masala ingredients in a blender and process to a fine paste.
✦ Spread half of the paste over the chicken and marinate for 1 hour.
✦ If using butter instead of ghee, you will need to clarify the butter. Melt the butter in a small saucepan over low heat. When the butter is simmering, continually skim off the froth until only clear liquid remains, about 3 to 5 minutes.
✦ Soak the saffron threads in the boiling water and set aside until ready to use.

COOKING   *45 minutes*
✦ Heat the ghee in a large, non-stick skillet over medium heat. Stir in the cinnamon and clove. Add the onions and cook until they are soft, about 3 minutes. Stir in the remaining masala paste, the strained saffron liquid, and add the chicken fillets.
✦ Cook over medium heat, turning the chicken so that both sides are coated with the sauce, for 10 minutes. When the ghee forms a separate layer on the surface, stir in the 3 tablespoons of water and bring the sauce to a boil.
✦ Reduce the heat and simmer, covered, until the chicken is tender, about 30 minutes.
✦ Remove the cinnamon stick.
✦ Transfer the chicken and sauce to a warm serving dish and serve with boiled rice.

PER SERVING

279 calories/1168 kilojoules; 32 g protein; 14 g fat, 46% of calories (8.6 g saturated, 28% of calories; 4.5 g monounsaturated, 15%; 0.9 g polyunsaturated, 3%); 5 g carbohydrate; 1.1 g dietary fiber; 195 mg sodium; 1 mg iron; 92 mg cholesterol.

Marinated Spiced Chicken

Chicken with Lentils and Vegetables

DHANSAK

This classic Parsi dish from the west coast of India combines lentils and vegetables in a spicy sauce, and is especially satisfying on a cold winter's day. Use yellow instead of red lentils if preferred.

SERVES 6

1 cup (6½ oz/200 g) red lentils
3 cups (24 fl oz/750 ml) water
1 teaspoon salt
2 tablespoons (1 oz/30 g)
   unsalted butter
½ teaspoon finely chopped ginger
1 onion, thinly sliced
2 garlic cloves, crushed
6 chicken breast fillets, about
   4 oz (125 g) each
1 small eggplant (aubergine), diced
⅔ cup (3 oz/100 g) winter
   squash (pumpkin), diced
1 large potato, diced
2 cups chopped spinach (English
   spinach)
1¾ cups (13 oz/410 g) coarsely
   chopped, canned tomatoes
   with their juice
2 tablespoons chopped mint
3 tablespoons chopped cilantro
   (coriander)

MASALA

2 tablespoons (1 oz/30 g)
   unsalted butter
1 large onion, finely sliced
½ teaspoon crushed ginger
3 garlic cloves, crushed
2 small red chilies, finely sliced
1 teaspoon ground turmeric
1 teaspoon ground coriander
½ teaspoon ground cinnamon
½ teaspoon ground cardamom
½ teaspoon ground cloves

PREPARATION   *1 hour and 20 minutes*

✦ Wash the lentils, cover in cold water and soak for 30 minutes. Drain. Transfer the lentils to a large saucepan and add the water and salt. Bring the lentils to a boil and skim off the froth. Simmer, uncovered, for 40 minutes. Drain the lentils, then add to a blender and purée.

COOKING   *1 hour*

✦ Heat the butter in a large skillet over medium heat. Add the ginger, onion and garlic and cook until the onion is soft, about 3 minutes. Add the chicken and cook until tender, about 20 minutes. Transfer the chicken mixture to a plate.

✦ Add the eggplant, winter squash, potato, spinach, tomatoes and their juice and the mint to the skillet. Cover, reduce the heat and simmer until the vegetables are tender, about 15 minutes. Set aside.

✦ To make the masala, heat the butter in a large saucepan over medium heat. Add the onion, ginger, garlic and chilies and cook for 2 minutes. Stir in the turmeric, ground coriander, cinnamon, cardamom and cloves and cook for 5 minutes.

✦ Stir in the puréed lentils and the vegetables and chicken and cook, stirring occasionally, until heated through, about 10 minutes.

✦ Place the chicken in a deep dish, spoon the lentils and vegetables on top and serve, garnished with the chopped cilantro.

PER SERVING

357 calories/1495 kilojoules; 40 g protein; 12 g fat, 31% of calories (6.3 g saturated, 16% of calories; 4.5 g monounsaturated, 12%; 1.2 g polyunsaturated, 3%); 21 g carbohydrate; 8.3 g dietary fiber; 456 mg sodium; 5.3 mg iron; 86 mg cholesterol.

Impressive fortifications like this dot the Indian landscape.

Chicken with Lentils and Vegetables

Chicken Curry

MURGH KARI

India is famous for its varied and inventive use of spices. The word "kari," from which curry is derived, means a sauce, and was originally used to describe sauces of a fairly liquid consistency. Many of today's curries are not so liquid.

SERVES 4

1 in (2.5 cm) ginger
1 large onion
1 tablespoon vegetable oil
1 lb (500 g) chicken breast fillets
2 garlic cloves, finely chopped
½ teaspoon cayenne pepper
½ teaspoon ground coriander
½ teaspoon ground cumin
½ teaspoon ground turmeric
¼ teaspoon fennel seeds, crushed
1¾ cups (13 oz/410 g) coarsely
    chopped, canned tomatoes
    with their juice
2 tablespoons chopped cilantro
    (coriander)
½ teaspoon garam masala
3 tablespoons plain yogurt
cilantro (coriander) leaves,
    for garnish
4 lemon wedges

PREPARATION *10 minutes*
♦ Peel and grate the ginger.
♦ Chop the onion.

COOKING *40 minutes*
♦ Heat the oil in a large skillet over medium heat. Add the chicken and cook until browned on both sides, about 5 minutes. Transfer to a plate.
♦ Add the onion, garlic and ginger and cook until the onion is soft, about 3 minutes. Stir in the cayenne pepper, ground coriander, cumin, turmeric and fennel seeds and cook for 1 minute. Stir in the tomatoes and their juice, the chopped cilantro and the garam masala.
♦ Return the chicken to the skillet and coat with the sauce. Bring to a boil, then reduce the heat, cover and simmer until the chicken is tender, about 25 minutes.
♦ Remove the skillet from the heat and stir in the yogurt.
♦ Place the chicken on a serving platter and spoon the sauce on top. Garnish with the cilantro leaves and lemon wedges and serve with rice.

PER SERVING
215 calories/899 kilojoules; 30 g protein; 7.4 g fat, 31% of calories (1.9 g saturated, 8% of calories; 2.9 g monounsaturated, 12%; 2.6 g polyunsaturated, 11%); 6 g carbohydrate; 2.3 g dietary fiber; 145 mg sodium; 1.6 mg iron; 64 mg cholesterol.

Red Chili Pepper Chicken

LAL MASALE WALI MURGH

This thick red sauce is traditional to the west coast of India. The color and texture come from the fresh red peppers combined with the ground almonds. Serve this dish with lime chutney and condiments of your choice.

SERVES 4

1 large onion, thinly sliced
1 in (2.5 cm) ginger, grated
2 tablespoons ground almonds
2 garlic cloves, chopped
2 red bell peppers (capsicum),
    chopped
1 tablespoon ground cumin
2 teaspoons ground coriander
1 teaspoon ground turmeric
½ teaspoon hot paprika
1 teaspoon salt
1 tablespoon vegetable oil
8 skinless chicken drumsticks,
    about 4 oz (125 g) each
½ cup (4 fl oz/125 ml) water
juice of 1 small lemon
mint sprigs, for garnish

PREPARATION *15 minutes*
♦ Place the onion, ginger, almonds, garlic, bell peppers, cumin, coriander, turmeric, paprika and salt in a blender and purée.

COOKING *40 minutes*
♦ Heat the oil in a large, non-stick skillet over low heat. Add the purée and cook, stirring frequently, for 10 minutes.
♦ Add the chicken, water and lemon juice and bring to a boil over medium heat. Reduce the heat, cover and simmer until the chicken is tender, about 25 minutes.

♦ Transfer to a serving dish and garnish with the mint sprigs. Serve with rice.

PER SERVING
256 calories/1070 kilojoules; 27 g protein; 14 g fat, 50% of calories (3.1 g saturated, 11% of calories; 6.8 g monounsaturated, 24.5%; 4.1 g polyunsaturated, 14.5%); 5 g carbohydrate; 2.6 g dietary fiber; 597 mg sodium; 2.3 mg iron; 103 mg cholesterol.

Red Chili Pepper Chicken

Roast Chicken and Yogurt

KOTOPOULO YIAOURTARA

Yogurt and cheeses of various types, particularly those made from sheep's and goat's milk, play an important part in Greek dishes. Here the combined yogurt and mint complement the oregano, lemon and olive oil—keynote flavors of the cuisine.

SERVES 6

1 cup (8 oz/250 g) low-fat plain yogurt
1 tablespoon chopped mint
1 tablespoon virgin olive oil
½ teaspoon grated lemon zest
juice of 1 lemon
½ teaspoon dried oregano
½ teaspoon freshly ground black pepper
1 chicken, about 3 lb (1.5 kg)
½ cup (4 fl oz/125 ml) dry white wine

PREPARATION   *15 minutes*

◆ Preheat the oven to 350°F (180°C).
◆ Place the yogurt in a small bowl and stir in the mint. Refrigerate.
◆ Combine the oil, lemon zest and juice, oregano and pepper in a small bowl. Brush the mixture over the chicken.
◆ Pour the wine into a roasting pan and place the chicken in the pan.

COOKING   *1 hour and 10 minutes plus 20 minutes standing time*

◆ Roast the chicken, basting frequently with the wine and cooking juices, until the juices run clear when the chicken is tested with a skewer, about 1 hour and 10 minutes.
◆ Cover and let stand for 20 minutes, then serve with the combined yogurt and mint and a crisp salad.

PER SERVING

276 calories/1156 kilojoules; 28 g protein; 15 g fat, 49% of calories (4.7 g saturated, 15% of calories; 8 g monounsaturated, 26%; 2.3 g polyunsaturated, 8%); 3 g carbohydrate; 0.4 g dietary fiber; 115 mg sodium; 1.1 mg iron; 84 mg cholesterol.

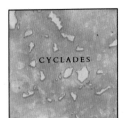

Chicken Pilaf

KOTOPOULO PILAFI

In Greek cuisine, rice is used mostly in stuffed vegetables and pilafs, which reflect the 300 plus years of Turkish rule. This pilaf has a very fresh Mediterranean flavor, which comes from the orange and lemon in the sauce.

SERVES 4

1 lb (500 g) boneless, skinless chicken thighs (thigh fillets)
2 tablespoons freshly squeezed lemon juice
1 tablespoon virgin olive oil
1 large onion, finely chopped
2 vine-ripened tomatoes, peeled and diced
1 tablespoon tomato paste
1/2 teaspoon ground cinnamon
1 teaspoon grated orange zest
juice of 1 orange
1½ cups (12 fl oz/375 ml) water
1¼ cups (8 1/2 oz/275 g) long-grain rice
2 bay leaves
salt, to taste
freshly ground black pepper, to taste
1 tablespoon finely chopped parsley

PREPARATION   *15 minutes plus 10 minutes marinating time*

◆ Cut the chicken into bite-sized pieces. Combine with the lemon juice in a small bowl and let stand for 10 minutes.

COOKING   *55 minutes*

◆ Heat the oil in a large, heavy-bottomed saucepan over medium-high heat. Add the chicken and cook until golden on all sides, about 4 minutes. Using a slotted spoon, transfer to a plate and set aside.
◆ Add the onion to the saucepan and cook until soft, about 3 minutes. Add the tomatoes and cook until soft, about 3 minutes.

◆ Return the chicken to the saucepan and stir in the tomato paste, cinnamon, orange zest and juice, water, rice and bay leaves. Add the salt and pepper. Bring to a boil, cover, reduce the heat and simmer until the rice is cooked, about 30 minutes.
◆ Place in a deep serving dish, garnish with the chopped parsley and serve.

PER SERVING

445 calories/1865 kilojoules; 28 g protein; 12 g fat, 23% of calories (3.3 g saturated, 6% of calories; 6.7 g monounsaturated, 13%; 2 g polyunsaturated, 4%); 57 g carbohydrate; 3.3 g dietary fiber; 110 mg sodium; 2.5 mg iron; 163 mg cholesterol.

Roast Chicken and Yogurt

Chicken with Okra

KOTOPOULO ME BAMYES

SERVES 4

8 oz (250 g) okra

2 tablespoons white wine vinegar

5 teaspoons virgin olive oil

8 boneless, skinless chicken
   thighs (thigh fillets), about
   2 oz (60 g) each

1 onion, finely chopped

2 garlic cloves, finely chopped

1¾ cups (13 oz/410 g) peeled
   and chopped tomatoes

1 tablespoon tomato paste

½ cup (4 fl oz/125 ml) dry
   white wine

1 tablespoon finely chopped
   flat-leaf parsley

1 bay leaf

½ teaspoon salt

¼ teaspoon freshly ground black
   pepper

1 cinnamon stick

flat-leaf parsley sprigs,
   for garnish

Okra is cultivated on a large scale in northern Greece. Often referred to as "ladies' fingers," okra needs to be handled with care. Do not cut the tops off too far from the stem or the glutinous juices will be released.

PREPARATION   *20 minutes*

◆ Cut the stems off the okra and discard. Place the okra in a dish and spoon the vinegar on top. Let stand for 10 minutes, then drain and set aside.

COOKING   *45 minutes*

◆ Heat 3 teaspoons of the oil in a large, non-stick skillet over medium-high heat. Add the chicken, in 2 batches if necessary, and brown on both sides, about 5 minutes per batch. Using a slotted spoon, transfer the chicken to a large saucepan.

◆ Add the remaining oil to the skillet. Add the onion and garlic and cook until the onion is soft, about 3 minutes. Stir in the tomatoes, tomato paste, wine, chopped parsley, bay leaf, salt and pepper. Cook until blended, about 2 minutes. Pour on top of the chicken, add the cinnamon stick and bring to a boil. Reduce the heat and simmer for 10 minutes.

◆ Add the okra and simmer for an additional 20 minutes. Transfer the chicken and sauce to a warm, deep serving dish, garnish with the parsley sprigs and serve with mashed potatoes.

PER SERVING

269 calories/1125 kilojoules; 26 g protein; 14 g fat, 46% of calories (3.6 g saturated, 12% of calories; 8.3 g monounsaturated, 27%; 2.1 g polyunsaturated, 7%); 6 g carbohydrate; 4.2 g dietary fiber; 361 mg sodium; 2.6 mg iron; 162 mg cholesterol.

The waters around the Greek islands are rich in seafood; this fishing boat is one of many plying its trade.

Chicken with Okra

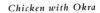

Chicken with Oregano

KOTOPOULO RIGANATO

SERVES 4

8 wooden skewers
1 lb (500 g) boneless, skinless
* chicken thighs (thigh fillets)*
2 tablespoons virgin olive oil
juice of 1 lemon
1 tablespoon chopped oregano
1 garlic clove, crushed
½ teaspoon salt
¼ teaspoon freshly ground black
* pepper*
oregano sprigs, for garnish

Oregano is native to the Mediterranean and has been used in Greek cooking since ancient times. Its scientific name, *Origanum*, comes from the Ancient Greek, and means "joy of the mountains." It grows wild on the rocky hills and mountainsides.

PREPARATION   *20 minutes plus at least 30 minutes soaking and marinating time*

◆ Soak the skewers in cold water for at least 30 minutes to prevent charring during cooking.
◆ Cut the chicken into bite-sized pieces.
◆ Combine the oil, lemon juice, oregano, garlic, salt and pepper in a large bowl. Add the chicken, cover and marinate in the refrigerator for 30 minutes.
◆ Preheat the broiler (grill).
◆ Thread the chicken pieces onto the skewers. Reserve and refrigerate the marinade.

COOKING   *10 minutes*

◆ Place the skewers under the broiler and broil (grill), basting frequently with the reserved marinade, until cooked through, about 4 minutes per side.
◆ Place on a warm serving dish, garnish with the sprigs of oregano and serve immediately with pita bread.

PER SERVING
229 calories/957 kilojoules; 23 g protein; 15 g fat, 58% of calories (3.7 g saturated, 14% of calories; 9.1 g monounsaturated, 35%; 2.2 g polyunsaturated, 9%); 2 g carbohydrate; 1 g dietary fiber; 324 mg sodium; 1.3 mg iron; 163 mg cholesterol.

Stewed Chicken with Tomatoes

KOTOPOULO KAPAMA

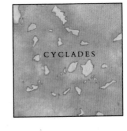

SERVES 4

12 oz (375 g) vine-ripened
* tomatoes*
1 lb (500 g) boneless, skinless
* chicken thighs (thigh fillets)*
1 teaspoon salt
½ teaspoon freshly ground black
* pepper*
1 tablespoon virgin olive oil
¾ cup (6 fl oz/180 ml) dry red
* wine*
½ cinnamon stick
¼ teaspoon ground allspice
2 cloves
1 bay leaf

Chickens in Greece are often allowed to range freely, and while the meat will be flavorful, it can also be tough. Simmering the chicken in a spiced broth makes the meat tender and also results in a spicy, aromatic sauce.

PREPARATION   *10 minutes*

◆ Place the tomatoes in a bowl and cover with boiling water. Let stand until the skin begins to split, about 10 minutes. Remove the tomatoes from the bowl, peel and chop.
◆ Sprinkle the chicken with the salt and pepper.

COOKING   *40 minutes*

◆ Heat the oil in a large, non-stick skillet over medium-high heat. Add the chicken and cook until golden on both sides, about 5 minutes. Using a slotted spoon, transfer the chicken to a plate.
◆ Pour the wine into the skillet. Add the remaining ingredients and bring to a boil over medium heat. Reduce the heat and simmer for 2 minutes.

◆ Return the chicken to the skillet and simmer until the chicken is cooked through and the sauce has reduced, about 20 minutes. Remove the bay leaf and discard.
◆ Place the chicken in a deep serving dish, spoon the sauce on top and serve with pasta or rice and green beans.

PER SERVING
236 calories/987 kilojoules; 24 g protein; 11 g fat, 42% of calories (3.1 g saturated, 11.8% of calories; 6.3 g monounsaturated, 23.9%; 1.6 g polyunsaturated, 6.3%); 3 g carbohydrate; 1.2 g dietary fiber; 579 mg sodium; 1.7 mg iron; 163 mg cholesterol.

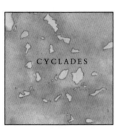

Chicken Pie

KOTOPETA

SERVES 6

3 tablespoons (1½ oz/45 g)
    butter, melted
1½ lb (750 g) boneless, skinless
    chicken thighs (thigh fillets)
1 lb (500 g) onions, thinly sliced
1¼ cups (10 fl oz/300 ml) water
1 teaspoon salt
⅔ cup (3 oz/90 g) freshly grated
    kefalotiri or Parmesan cheese
2 tablespoons finely chopped
    parsley
¼ teaspoon ground nutmeg
4 large eggs, beaten
14 sheets phyllo pastry
herb sprigs, for garnish

This light and delicate pie enclosed in tissue-thin Greek phyllo pastry is an ideal dish for lunch or a picnic. The slow simmering of the onions brings out their flavor, which combines well with the classic filling of eggs and cheese.

PREPARATION   *15 minutes*
✦ Grease a 12 × 9 × 2 in (30 × 20 × 5 cm) baking dish with some of the melted butter.

COOKING   *2 hours and 20 minutes*
✦ Place the chicken fillets and onions in a large saucepan. Add the water and salt and bring to a boil. Reduce the heat and simmer, covered, for 20 minutes. Using a slotted spoon, remove the chicken, cool and then shred.
✦ Meanwhile, continue simmering the onions, uncovered, until the mixture reduces to a thick sauce, about 45 minutes.
✦ Remove the saucepan from the heat and stir in the chicken, cheese, parsley and nutmeg. Let cool for 10 minutes, then stir in the eggs.
✦ Preheat the oven to 375°F (190°C).

✦ Line the base of the baking dish with 7 sheets of the pastry, brushing each sheet with some of the melted butter. Allow the pastry to hang over the edges of the dish. Spread the filling evenly over the pastry and fold over the overhanging sides.
✦ Cover with the remaining sheets of pastry, brushing each layer, and the top, with the remaining butter. Fold over any overlapping pastry. Bake until golden, about 40 minutes.
✦ Garnish with the herb sprigs and serve with a salad or vegetables of your choice.

PER SERVING
436 calories/1824 kilojoules; 36 g protein; 23 g fat,
47% of calories (11.5 g saturated, 23.5% of calories;
8.7 g monounsaturated, 17.9%; 2.8 g polyunsaturated, 5.6%);
23 g carbohydrate; 1.8 g dietary fiber; 909 mg sodium;
2.5 mg iron; 314 mg cholesterol.

The tranquil waters around the island of Santorini, a popular tourist destination.

Chicken Pie

Chicken with Lemons
KOTOPOULO LEMONATO

SERVES 4

1 large lemon
6 cloves
extra virgin olive oil, to cover
    the lemon
1 tablespoon virgin olive oil
1 tablespoon (½ oz/15 g) butter
8 chicken thighs, about 4 oz
    (125 g) each, skin removed
½ teaspoon salt
¼ teaspoon freshly ground black
    pepper
4 shallots (French shallots),
    sliced
½ cup (2½ oz/75 g) pitted
    black olives
1 cup (8 fl oz/250 ml) chicken
    stock, skimmed of fat
1 tablespoon chopped thyme
thyme sprigs, for garnish

Preserved lemons usually need to cure for about two weeks. In this quicker variation, a lemon is studded with cloves and marinated in olive oil for two days. The lemon loses its sharpness and develops a soft texture.

PREPARATION   *25 minutes plus 2 days marinating time*
✦ Place the lemon in a small saucepan and cover with cold water. Bring to a boil, then reduce the heat and simmer for 15 minutes. Remove from the water and pat dry carefully with kitchen towels. Press the cloves gently into the lemon and place in a jar. Cover with the extra virgin olive oil, seal well and leave to marinate at room temperature for 2 days.
✦ Remove the cloves from the lemon and discard. Cut the lemon into 8 wedges.

COOKING   *1 hour*
✦ Heat the virgin olive oil and butter in a large, non-stick skillet over medium-high heat. Sprinkle the chicken with the salt and pepper. Add to the skillet in 2 batches and cook until golden on both sides, about 3 minutes per batch. Using a slotted spoon, transfer the chicken to a plate.

✦ Add the shallots to the skillet and cook until golden, about 5 minutes. Return the chicken to the skillet, and stir in the olives and stock. Bring to a boil over medium heat, then reduce the heat and simmer for 25 minutes.
✦ Add the lemon wedges and chopped thyme and simmer, stirring occasionally, for an additional 15 minutes.
✦ Place the chicken in a deep serving dish and spoon the sauce on top. Garnish with the thyme sprigs and serve with crusty bread and a salad.

PER SERVING
268 calories/1124 kilojoules; 23 g protein; 18 g fat, 61% of calories (5.7 g saturated, 20% of calories; 10.1 g monounsaturated, 34%; 2.2 g polyunsaturated, 7%); 3 g carbohydrate; 2.4 g dietary fiber; 869 mg sodium; 1.3 mg iron; 170 mg cholesterol.

Chicken with Mustard Sauce
KOTOPOULO ME MOUSTARDA SALTSA

SERVES 6

juice of 2 large lemons
¼ cup (2 fl oz/60 ml) plus
    1 teaspoon virgin olive oil
2 garlic cloves, finely chopped
1 chicken, about 3 lb (1.5 kg)
1 tablespoon mild mustard
2 teaspoons chopped thyme

The combination of lemon, olive oil and thyme gives this dish a true Greek flavor. It is important to stir the sauce continuously during cooking. It will separate on standing, so prepare it close to the end of cooking time and serve immediately.

PREPARATION   *10 minutes*
✦ Preheat the oven to 350°F (180°C).
✦ Combine 1 tablespoon of the lemon juice, 1 teaspoon of the olive oil and the garlic in a small bowl. Brush half of the mixture over the chicken.

COOKING   *1 hour and 30 minutes*
✦ Place the chicken on a rack in a roasting pan. Roast, basting occasionally with the remaining lemon mixture, until the juices run clear when the chicken is tested with a skewer in the thigh, about 1½ hours. Place the chicken on a serving platter and keep warm.
✦ Meanwhile, prepare the sauce. Mix the remaining

lemon juice with the mustard, the remaining oil and the thyme in a small saucepan. Bring to a boil over low heat, then simmer, stirring continuously, until thoroughly blended and smooth, about 3 minutes.
✦ Pour the sauce on top of the chicken and serve immediately with steamed vegetables.

PER SERVING
231 calories/967 kilojoules; 25 g protein; 14 g fat, 53% of calories (4.6 g saturated, 17.6% of calories; 7.1 g monounsaturated, 27%; 2.3 g polyunsaturated, 8.4%); 1 g carbohydrate; 1.2 g dietary fiber; 107 mg sodium; 1.1 mg iron; 83 mg cholesterol.

Chicken with Lemons

Chicken with Noodles

KOTOPOULO ME HILOPITTES

SERVES 6

6 chicken pieces, about 3 lb
    (1.5 kg), skin removed
salt, to taste
freshly ground black pepper,
    to taste
2 tablespoons virgin olive oil
1 onion, finely chopped
1¾ cups (13 oz / 410 g) coarsely
    chopped, canned tomatoes
    with their juice
½ cup (4 fl oz / 125 ml) dry red
    wine
2 teaspoons chopped oregano
1 bay leaf
12 oz (375 g) noodles
⅓ cup (1½ oz / 45 g) freshly
    grated kefalotiri or Parmesan
    cheese

This is simple family fare from the Peloponnese, the southern part of Greece, which is separated from the rest of the country by the Corinth Canal. The Greeks like their chicken—and all their meat—cooked until it is falling off the bone.

PREPARATION   *10 minutes*
✦ Season the chicken pieces with the salt and pepper.

COOKING   *1 hour and 25 minutes*
✦ Heat the oil in a large, heavy-bottomed saucepan over medium-high heat. Add the chicken in 2 batches and cook until golden on all sides, about 5 minutes per batch. Remove from the saucepan and set aside.
✦ Add the onion to the saucepan and cook until golden, about 5 minutes. Return the chicken pieces to the saucepan and stir in the tomatoes and their juice, the wine, oregano and bay leaf. Bring to a boil, then reduce the heat, cover and simmer until the chicken is very tender, about 1 hour.

✦ Meanwhile, bring a large saucepan of water to a boil. Add the noodles and cook until tender, about 10 minutes. Drain well.
✦ When the chicken is cooked, remove from the saucepan and keep warm. Remove the bay leaf and discard. Stir the cheese into the sauce.
✦ To serve, arrange the noodles on a large platter and top with the chicken. Spoon the sauce on top.

PER SERVING
452 calories / 1892 kilojoules; 37 g protein; 12 g fat, 24% of calories (4 g saturated, 7.9% of calories; 6.4 g monounsaturated, 12.7%; 1.6 g polyunsaturated, 3.4%); 44 g carbohydrate; 4 g dietary fiber; 400 mg sodium; 2.3 mg iron; 82 mg cholesterol.

A fruit and vegetable seller on Mykonos makes a sale; his donkey carries the produce.

Grilled Chicken Padang-Style

SINGGANG AYAM

SERVES 4

*4 chicken breast fillets, about
    4 oz (125 g) each
1 cup (8 fl oz/250 ml) chicken
    stock, skimmed of fat
1 stalk lemongrass, cut into
    3 pieces
1 kaffir lime leaf or lime leaf
1 cup (8 fl oz/250 ml) coconut
    milk*

CHILI PASTE

*1 tablespoon sesame oil
1 large onion, finely chopped
2 garlic cloves, finely chopped
2 red chilies, finely chopped
1 in (2.5 cm) ginger, thinly sliced
½ in (1 cm) galangal, thinly
    sliced
½ teaspoon ground turmeric
1 tablespoon water*

This is an everyday dish from West Sumatra. The chilies typically used in Padang
are not the small hot chilies but the larger, milder red ones. Kaffir lime leaves
are available from specialty Asian food stores.

PREPARATION   *20 minutes*
✦ Place the chicken fillets between 2 pieces of plastic
wrap and flatten to an even thickness with a meat
mallet.

COOKING   *40 minutes*
✦ Heat the oil in a large, non-stick skillet over low
heat. Add the chili paste ingredients and cook, stirring,
until the onion and ginger are soft, about 3 minutes.
Transfer to a food processor and blend until smooth.
✦ Spread the paste evenly over the top of each chicken
fillet, then place in the skillet in a single layer.
✦ Carefully pour the chicken stock around the chicken,
making sure that the stock does not cover the paste.
Add the lemongrass and kaffir lime leaf and bring to
a boil. Reduce the heat and simmer until the chicken
is cooked through, about 20 minutes.

✦ Meanwhile, preheat the broiler (grill).
✦ Remove the cooked chicken from the skillet, place
under the broiler and cook until the paste turns into
a soft crust, about 5 minutes. Transfer the chicken to
a warm serving platter.
✦ Meanwhile, add the coconut milk to the cooking
liquid in the skillet and simmer until the sauce has
reduced and thickened, about 5 minutes. Discard the
lemongrass and kaffir lime leaf. Pour the sauce into a
small bowl.
✦ Serve the chicken with the sauce and boiled rice.

PER SERVING
*283 calories/1183 kilojoules; 30 g protein; 15 g fat, 48% of
calories (9.2 g saturated, 30% of calories; 3.5 g monounsaturated,
11%; 2.3 g polyunsaturated, 7%); 6 g carbohydrate; 2 g dietary
fiber; 303 mg sodium; 1.7 mg iron; 63 mg cholesterol.*

*Bananas ripening
in the sun have
proved irresistible
to these Indonesian
children!*

Javanese Spiced Chicken

AYAM BENGGANG

SPICE PASTE

1 onion, finely chopped
2 small red chilies, seeded and
    sliced
2 garlic cloves, finely chopped
1 stalk lemongrass, thinly sliced
1 clove
½ in (1 cm) galangal, thinly sliced
1 teaspoon ground coriander
½ teaspoon cardamom seeds
½ teaspoon ground cinnamon
½ teaspoon ground cumin
¼ teaspoon freshly ground black
    pepper
¼ teaspoon nutmeg
¼ teaspoon ground turmeric
2 tablespoons fresh lime juice
2 tablespoons water
2 teaspoons sesame oil
1 teaspoon shrimp paste

4 cups spinach (English spinach),
    washed and trimmed
1 chicken, about 3 lb (1.5 kg)
parsley sprigs, for garnish

This recipe originated in the area around Banten in western Java. There the leaves of the cassava, a hardy plant that grows along the roadside, would be used in the stuffing. Elsewhere, spinach makes a good substitute.

PREPARATION   *20 minutes plus*
                  several hours standing time

✦ Combine the spice paste ingredients in a blender and purée until smooth.
✦ Chop and blanch the spinach. Place in a bowl, add half of the paste and mix together.
✦ Loosen the skin of the chicken and spread the spinach mixture under the skin over the breast. Spread the remaining paste over the chicken skin. Wrap the chicken in aluminum foil and refrigerate for several hours, or overnight.
✦ Just before cooking, preheat the oven to 350°F (180°C).

COOKING   *1 hour and 40 minutes*

✦ Place the wrapped chicken on a rack in a roasting pan. Bake for 1 hour, then open the foil and roast until the juices run clear when the chicken is tested with a

skewer in the thigh, about 30 minutes. Carefully remove the chicken from the foil, reserving the cooking juices, and place on a warm serving platter. Garnish with the parsley.
✦ Pour the cooking juices into a small saucepan. Skim off the fat and discard. Simmer for 3 minutes. Serve as a sauce with the chicken, accompanied by rice or vegetables.

PER SERVING
240 calories/1005 kilojoules; 26 g protein; 15 g fat, 53% of calories (4.8 g saturated, 17% of calories; 7 g monounsaturated, 25%; 3.2 g polyunsaturated, 11%); 1 g carbohydrate; 1.3 g dietary fiber; 85 mg sodium; 2.1 mg iron; 84 mg cholesterol.

For an Indonesian meal, all the dishes are served together, rather than as separate courses. This gathering is at Denpasar on the island of Bali.

Javanese Spiced Chicken

Hot Dry Chicken Curry with Sumatra Chili

RENDANG AYAM

SERVES 4

1 stalk lemongrass
4 cups (32 fl oz / 1 l) coconut milk
1 large onion, finely chopped
2 garlic cloves, finely chopped
2 teaspoons sambal ulek
    (Indonesian chili sauce)
1 in (2.5 cm) galangal, grated
1 teaspoon salt
½ teaspoon ground turmeric
4 chicken leg-thigh quarters
    (chicken Marylands), skin
    removed

Beef *rendang* is a classic Sumatran dish and is usually a dry curry. As chicken cooks more quickly than red meat, this dish retains some of the lovely sauce. The amount of coconut milk needed results in a high level of fat.

PREPARATION   *10 minutes*
✦ Cut the lemongrass into 4 pieces and crush slightly.

COOKING   *1 hour and 50 minutes*
✦ Place all the ingredients except the chicken in a large saucepan. Bring to a boil over medium heat, then lower the heat and simmer until the liquid has reduced by half, about 1 hour.
✦ Add the chicken, cover and cook for 20 minutes.

Remove the lid and cook until the chicken is cooked through, about 25 minutes.
✦ Place the chicken on a deep serving platter, spoon the sauce on top and serve with boiled rice.

PER SERVING
560 calories/2344 kilojoules; 29 g protein; 42 g fat, 68% of calories (34 g saturated, 55% of calories; 6 g monounsaturated, 9.6%; 2 g polyunsaturated, 3.4%); 16 g carbohydrate; 0.7 g dietary fiber; 572 mg sodium; 1.4 mg iron; 104 mg cholesterol.

Chicken in Coconut Milk Sauce

OPOR AYAM

SERVES 4

4 chicken breasts, about 8 oz
    (250 g) each, skin removed
1 tablespoon freshly squeezed
    lime juice
1 tablespoon vegetable oil
1½ cups (12 fl oz / 375 ml)
    coconut milk
1 kaffir lime leaf or lime leaf
1 bay leaf
¼ cup cilantro (coriander) leaves

SPICE PASTE

1 onion, finely chopped
3 garlic cloves, chopped
2 tablespoons blanched almonds
½ teaspoon freshly ground black
    pepper
½ teaspoon ground coriander
½ teaspoon ground cumin
½ in (1.25 cm) galangal, grated
½ teaspoon salt
¼ cup (2 fl oz / 60 ml) coconut
    milk

Coconut palms line the shores of virtually every Indonesian island, so it is not surprising that coconut milk is one of the main ingredients in Indonesian cooking. Local cooks use fresh coconut milk, but the canned variety gives a good result.

PREPARATION   *10 minutes*
✦ Rub the chicken breasts with the lime juice.
✦ Combine the spice paste ingredients in a blender and purée until smooth.

COOKING   *50 minutes*
✦ Heat the oil in a large, non-stick skillet over medium-high heat. Add the chicken and brown, about 3 minutes per side. Remove from the skillet and set aside.
✦ Add the paste to the skillet and cook, stirring continuously, for 5 minutes. Return the chicken to the skillet and add the coconut milk and kaffir lime and bay leaves. Reduce the heat and simmer, uncovered,

until the chicken is cooked through, about 30 minutes. Remove the kaffir lime and bay leaves. Stir in the cilantro leaves.
✦ Transfer the dish to a warm serving platter. Serve with boiled rice.

PER SERVING
386 calories/1616 kilojoules; 32 g protein; 25 g fat, 58% of calories (15.3 g saturated, 35.4% of calories; 5.9 g monounsaturated, 13.9%; 3.8 g polyunsaturated, 8.7%); 8 g carbohydrate; 3.1 g dietary fiber; 318 mg sodium; 2.3 mg iron; 63 mg cholesterol.

Chicken in Coconut Milk Sauce

Manado Chicken with Hot Chilies

AYAM RICA RICA

Rica rica is traditionally a very hot and spicy dish. This is a milder version but you can always add more chilies according to taste, or add more onions and fewer chilies if you prefer an even milder dish.

SERVES 6

CHILI PASTE

2 tablespoons water

1 tablespoon sunflower oil

1 large onion, chopped

3 small red chilies, halved and seeded

2 garlic cloves

1 in (2.5 cm) ginger, finely chopped

½ teaspoon shrimp paste

1 chicken, about 3 lb (1.5 kg), skin removed

1 tablespoon freshly squeezed lime juice

½ teaspoon salt

PREPARATION   *25 minutes*

✦ Combine the chili paste ingredients in a blender and purée until smooth. Place in a small saucepan and cook over low heat, stirring occasionally, for 5 minutes. Remove from the heat and cool, about 10 minutes.

✦ Meanwhile, preheat the oven to 350°F (180°C).

✦ Split the chicken down the backbone. Press down firmly with the palm of your hand to flatten. Rub the chicken with the lime juice and salt. Spread the cooled paste over the chicken, then wrap in aluminum foil with the seam upwards.

COOKING   *1 hour and 5 minutes*

✦ Place the chicken on a rack in a roasting pan and bake for 30 minutes. Open the foil and cook until the juices run clear when the chicken is tested with a skewer in the thigh, about 30 minutes. Remove the chicken carefully from the foil, reserving the juices.

✦ Cut into serving portions and place on a serving platter. Pour the cooking juices on top of the chicken. Serve with rice.

PER SERVING

177 calories/739 kilojoules; 28 g protein; 6.6 g fat, 33% of calories (1.7 g saturated, 8.6% of calories; 2.7 g monounsaturated, 13.5%; 2.2 g polyunsaturated, 10.9%); 2 g carbohydrate; 0.8 g dietary fiber; 248 mg sodium; 1.3 mg iron; 75 mg cholesterol.

A Javanese market scene.

One Pot Chicken

MIZU-TAKI

Mizu-taki literally means "water simmered." A stock is prepared on the stove top, then transferred to a pot on the table to continue cooking. The diners add chunks of chicken and vegetables to the stock and then dip them into a sauce.

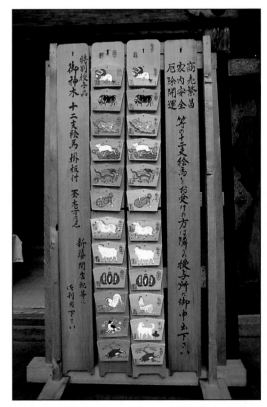

Asahikawa
Kushiro
Sapporo
Obihiro
Muroran
HOKKAIDŌ

SERVES 6

PONZU SAUCE

¼ cup (2 fl oz / 60 ml) freshly squeezed lime juice

2 tablespoons sake (rice wine)

¼ cup (2 fl oz / 60 ml) dark soy sauce

1½ teaspoons tamari sauce

1 tablespoon mirin (sweet rice wine)

¼ cup dried bonito (tuna) flakes

1 in (2.5 cm) strip kombu (dried kelp)

GINGER SOY SAUCE

1 tablespoon grated ginger

¼ cup (2 fl oz / 60 ml) dark soy sauce

3 oz (90 g) dried harusame (Japanese cellophane) noodles

3 in (7.5 cm) square piece kombu (dried kelp)

3 stalks bok choy, chopped

3 oz (90 g) shiitake mushrooms

2 carrots, cut into julienne strips

1½ lb (750 g) boneless, skinless chicken thighs (thigh fillets)

8 cups (64 fl oz / 2 l) water

wasabi paste (Japanese horseradish), for serving

PREPARATION *30 minutes plus at least 24 hours refrigerating time (for sauce)*

◆ To make the ponzu sauce, combine the ingredients in a jar and refrigerate for 24 hours. Strain and refrigerate until required. Any leftover sauce will keep for up to 12 months.

◆ To prepare the ginger soy sauce, mix together the ginger and soy sauce in a small bowl.

◆ Soak the noodles in hot water for 10 minutes, then drain.

◆ Wipe the surface of the kombu lightly, then slash it several times.

◆ Arrange the bok choy, mushrooms and carrots on a serving platter. Cover and refrigerate.

◆ Cut the chicken into bite-sized pieces.

COOKING *20 minutes*

◆ Place the chicken, water and kombu in a large saucepan and bring to a boil. Remove the kombu as soon as the water boils and discard. Reduce the heat and simmer for 10 minutes. Using a slotted spoon, transfer the chicken to a warm serving platter.

◆ Place the hot cooking liquid in a fondue pot, electric saucepan or electric wok on the table and bring to a simmer. Place the bowls of ginger soy sauce and ponzu sauce on the table. Bring the platters of prepared vegetables and cooked chicken to the table—

each diner adds a selection of these to the stock—they are simmered for 2 to 3 minutes, then removed with chopsticks or scoops to the individual plate.

◆ When all the chicken and vegetables have been cooked, add the noodles to the broth and simmer until heated through, about 1 to 2 minutes.

◆ Serve the noodles in individual bowls, with the wasabi paste on the side.

PER SERVING

225 calories / 941 kilojoules; 27 g protein; 8.7 g fat, 34% of calories (3.2 g saturated, 12.6% of calories; 4.1 g monounsaturated, 16%; 1.4 g polyunsaturated, 5.4%); 8 g carbohydrate; 3.7 g dietary fiber; 1026 mg sodium; 2 mg iron; 165 mg cholesterol.

Japanese calligraphy and stylized illustration make up this attractive board.

Chicken Teriyaki

TORI NO TERIYAKI

SERVES 4

8 chicken thighs, about 4 oz
(250 g) each
1 tablespoon vegetable oil
herbs, for garnish

TERIYAKI SAUCE

3 tablespoons mirin (sweet rice
wine)
3 tablespoons sake (rice wine)
3 tablespoons reduced-sodium,
dark soy sauce
1½ teaspoons sugar

This dish combines the flavors of mirin and sake, which are often used in Japanese cuisine. Mirin is a sweet rice wine that is used for flavoring dishes and in glazing sauces. Use pale sweet sherry if it is unavailable. Sake is Japan's famous rice wine.

PREPARATION   *20 minutes*
◆ Using a small sharp knife, carefully remove the bone from the chicken thighs. Pierce the skin of the chicken with a fork.
◆ Combine the teriyaki sauce ingredients in a small bowl.

COOKING   *40 minutes*
◆ Heat the oil in a large, non-stick skillet over medium-high heat. Add the chicken, skin side down, and cook until the skin is golden, about 5 minutes. Reduce the heat to low, turn the chicken and cook until cooked through, about 20 minutes. Remove the chicken from the skillet.
◆ Add the teriyaki sauce and stir to combine with the skillet juices and scrapings from bottom of the pan.

Bring to a boil over medium heat. Return the chicken to the skillet, reduce the heat to low and turn the chicken to coat evenly with the sauce. Cook until the sauce has reduced by two-thirds, about 3 to 5 minutes. Remove the chicken, slice and arrange on a platter and spoon the sauce on top. Garnish with the herbs and serve accompanied by steamed rice.

PER SERVING
299 calories/1251 kilojoules; 21 g protein; 20 g fat,
58% of calories (6.1 g saturated, 18% of calories;
9.8 g monounsaturated, 28%; 4.1 g polyunsaturated, 12%);
5 g carbohydrate; 0 g dietary fiber; 456 mg sodium; 1.3 mg iron;
188 mg cholesterol.

Yuan-Style Grilled Chicken

TORI NO YUAN-YAKI

SERVES 4

8 chicken thighs, about 4 oz
(250 g) each

MARINADE

3 tablespoons mirin (sweet rice
wine)
3 tablespoons sake (rice wine)
3 tablespoons reduced-sodium,
dark soy sauce
grated zest of 1 lime
¼ teaspoon sansho pepper

Soy sauce was taken to Japan by the Chinese but the Japanese then adapted the fermenting process to produce a lighter and sweeter sauce. Even the Japanese dark soy sauce is in general lighter than the Chinese soy sauces.

PREPARATION   *5 minutes plus 1 hour marinating time*
◆ Using a small sharp knife, carefully remove the bone from the chicken thighs.
◆ Place the marinade ingredients in a large bowl and combine well. Add the chicken, stir to coat, cover and refrigerate for 1 hour.
◆ Preheat the broiler (grill).
◆ Remove the chicken from the marinade, reserving the marinade.

COOKING   *10 minutes*
◆ Place the chicken under the broiler, baste with the marinade, cook until the skin is crisp and the chicken

is cooked through, about 5 minutes on each side. Place the chicken pieces on a serving platter and serve with rice.

PER SERVING
263 calories/1100 kilojoules; 21 g protein; 16.3 g fat, 55% of
calories (5.6 g saturated, 19% of calories; 8.6 g monounsaturated,
29%; 2.1 g polyunsaturated, 7%); 4 g carbohydrate; 0.1 g dietary
fiber; 455 mg sodium; 1.2 mg iron; 188 mg cholesterol.

Skewered Chicken

YAKITORI

SERVES 4

8 wooden skewers
1 lb (500 g) skinless, boneless
  chicken thighs (thigh fillets)
½ red bell pepper (capsicum)
3 scallions (spring onions)

MARINADE

¼ cup (2 fl oz/60 ml) reduced-
  sodium, dark soy sauce
2 tablespoons sake (rice wine)
1 tablespoon mirin (sweet rice
  wine)
2 teaspoons superfine (caster)
  sugar

This is a favorite dish at *Teppan Yaki*, or mixed grill restaurants. However, *yakitori* is also ideal for cooking under the broiler or on the barbecue at home. The sugar in the marinade helps give the broiled chicken a deep golden color.

PREPARATION   *20 minutes plus 30 minutes soaking time, cooling and marinating*

✦ Soak the skewers in water for at least 30 minutes to prevent charring during cooking.
✦ Place the marinade ingredients in a small saucepan and bring to a boil over medium-high heat. Reduce the heat and simmer for 3 minutes to burn off the alcohol. Remove from the heat and let cool completely, about 20 minutes.
✦ Chop the chicken into bite-sized pieces. Cut the pepper into ½ in (1 cm) squares and the scallions into 1 in (2.5 cm) lengths. Thread the chicken, peppers and scallions alternately onto the skewers and place in a shallow dish.
✦ Pour the marinade on top of the skewers, and marinate in the refrigerator for 10 minutes.

✦ Meanwhile, preheat the broiler (grill) or prepare the barbecue.

COOKING   *10 minutes*

✦ Remove the chicken from the marinade, reserving the marinade in the refrigerator. Broil the chicken, basting with the marinade, until golden, about 3 to 5 minutes per side. Place on a serving platter and serve the chicken on a bed of rice.

PER SERVING
198 calories/828 kilojoules; 24 g protein; 7.5 g fat, 34% of calories (2.5 g saturated, 11% of calories; 3.7 g monounsaturated, 17%; 1.3 g polyunsaturated, 6%); 7 g carbohydrate; 0.2 g dietary fiber; 605 mg sodium; 1.3 mg iron; 163 mg cholesterol.

*A fine example
of one of Kyoto's
many shrines.*

Skewered Chicken

Steamed Chicken in Seasoned Broth
TORINIKU SHIOMUSHI

SERVES 6

1 chicken, about 3 lb (1.5 kg)
1 cup (8 fl oz/250 ml) water
3 tablespoons sake (rice wine)
3 tablespoons mirin (sweet rice wine)
¼ teaspoon salt
1½ tablespoons reduced-sodium, dark soy sauce
juice of 1 small lemon
1 teaspoon sansho pepper

This typical Japanese dish with its light, subtle flavors is enhanced by sansho pepper. Sansho pepper comes from the prickly ash and is a greenish brown, ground spice with a lemony flavor. Sansho pepper is available from specialty Asian food stores.

PREPARATION   *10 minutes*
✦ Using poultry shears, cut the chicken into 6 pieces.
✦ Pour the water into the base of a steamer and place the chicken on the steaming rack. Sprinkle with the salt. Combine the sake, mirin and salt and pour on top of the chicken.

COOKING   *55 minutes*
✦ Cover the steamer and bring to a boil over medium heat. Reduce the heat and simmer until the chicken is cooked through, about 40 minutes. Transfer to a warm serving bowl and keep warm.

✦ Strain the cooking liquid and reserve ¾ cup (6 fl oz/180 ml). Put the reserved cooking liquid in a small saucepan, add the soy sauce and lemon juice and bring to a boil over low heat. Simmer for 5 minutes, then pour on top of the chicken. Sprinkle with the sansho pepper and serve with a medley of steamed vegetables.

PER SERVING
238 calories/997 kilojoules; 25 g protein; 13 g fat, 48% of calories (4.4 g saturated, 16.3% of calories; 6.4 g monounsaturated, 23.5%; 2.2 g polyunsaturated, 8.2%); 2 g carbohydrate; 0.4 g dietary fiber; 380 mg sodium; 1 mg iron; 83 mg cholesterol.

Fried Chicken
TATSUTAAGE

SERVES 4

1 lb (500 g) boneless, skinless chicken thighs (thigh fillets)
¼ cup (2 fl oz/60 ml) reduced-sodium, dark soy sauce
3 tablespoons mirin (sweet rice wine)
2 teaspoons sugar
1 teaspoon dried basil
¼ teaspoon salt
2 sheets toasted nori (dried seaweed)
½ cup (1 oz/30 g) cornstarch (cornflour)
3 tablespoons vegetable oil
wasabi paste (Japanese horseradish), for serving

Nori, the dried seaweed used as a wrapper for *sushi*, has a delicate ocean taste that is very popular in Japan. It is sold in thin flat sheets, plain or toasted, by specialty Asian food stores. This dish is perfect for lunch or as finger food for a party.

PREPARATION   *35 minutes*
✦ Cut the chicken into bite-sized pieces.
✦ Combine the soy sauce, mirin, sugar, basil and salt in a large bowl. Add the chicken and marinate for 20 minutes. Remove the chicken from the marinade and drain well.
✦ Crumble the nori finely. Combine with the cornstarch in a clean, plastic bag. Add the chicken pieces and coat with the flour mixture. Shake to remove the excess flour.

COOKING   *10 minutes*
✦ Heat half of the oil in a medium, non-stick skillet over medium-high heat. Add half of the chicken and

cook until golden, about 5 minutes. Transfer to a serving platter and keep warm. Heat the remaining oil and cook the remaining chicken in the same manner.
✦ Serve hot, with the wasabi paste, accompanied by a green salad.

PER SERVING
343 calories/1435 kilojoules; 24 g protein; 18 g fat, 47% of calories (3.9 g saturated, 10.3% of calories; 6.9 g monounsaturated, 17.9%; 7.2 g polyunsaturated, 18.8%); 19 g carbohydrate; 0.1 g dietary fiber; 745 mg sodium; 1.3 mg iron; 162 mg cholesterol.

Chicken Cacciatore with Black Olive and Anchovy Sauce

POLLO ALLA CACCIATORA CON LE OLIVE

SERVES 4

2 canned anchovy fillets
1 tablespoon milk
1½ tablespoons all-purpose
    (plain) flour
1 teaspoon dried oregano
¼ teaspoon salt
¼ teaspoon freshly ground black
    pepper
8 boneless, skinless chicken
    thighs (thigh fillets), about
    2 oz (60 g) each
1½ tablespoons virgin olive oil
1 onion, finely chopped
2 garlic cloves, finely chopped
¼ cup (2 fl oz/60 ml) dry
    white wine
1 tablespoon white wine vinegar
1 cup (8 fl oz/250 ml) chicken
    stock, skimmed of fat
3 large, vine-ripened tomatoes,
    peeled and chopped
2 tablespoons shredded basil
1 bay leaf
2 tablespoons sliced, pitted black
    olives

Pollo alla cacciatora is one of the Italian dishes that has become popular all over the world. *Alla cacciatora* means "hunter's style," and it indicates a dish of poultry or game braised in a sauce of tomatoes, onions and wine.

PREPARATION   *20 minutes*

✦ Soak the anchovies in the milk for 10 minutes, then drain and pat dry with paper towels. Coarsely chop the anchovies.

✦ Combine the flour, oregano, salt and pepper on a plate. Coat the chicken in the seasoned flour and shake off the excess flour.

COOKING   *45 minutes*

✦ Heat 1 tablespoon of the oil in a large, non-stick skillet over high heat. Add the chicken in 2 batches and cook until browned, about 5 minutes per batch. Remove from the skillet and set aside.

✦ Add the remaining oil to the skillet. Add the onion and garlic and cook, stirring occasionally, until the onion is soft, about 3 minutes. Stir in the wine and vinegar and bring to a boil. Reduce the heat and simmer until reduced by half.

✦ Add the chicken stock and return to a boil. Return the chicken to the skillet, add the tomatoes, basil and bay leaf and simmer until the chicken is cooked through, about 15 minutes. Remove the chicken to a warm serving dish.

✦ Add the olives and anchovies to the skillet, stir and cook for 2 minutes. Pour the sauce on top of the chicken and serve with rice.

PER SERVING

256 calories/1070 kilojoules; 24 g protein; 14 g fat, 48% of calories (3.7 g saturated, 12.5% of calories; 8.2 g monounsaturated, 28.3%; 2.1 g polyunsaturated, 7.2%); 6 g carbohydrate; 0.8 g dietary fiber; 613 mg sodium; 1.9 mg iron; 164 mg cholesterol.

Chicken Cacciatore Maddalena

POLLO ALLA CACCIATORA ALLA MADDALENA

SERVES 6

1 stalk celery
2 garlic cloves
1 tablespoon virgin olive oil
6 chicken breast fillets, about
    4 oz (125 g) each
½ cup (4 fl oz/125 ml) dry
    white wine
2 bay leaves
½ teaspoon salt
¼ teaspoon freshly ground
    black pepper
2 tablespoons finely chopped
    flat-leaf parsley

Sometimes it seems as if every Italian cook has a different recipe for chicken cacciatore. This one is unusual in that there are no tomatoes in the ingredients, and it is very quick and easy to prepare.

PREPARATION   *5 minutes*

✦ Finely chop the celery and garlic.

COOKING   *40 minutes*

✦ Heat the oil in a large, non-stick skillet over medium-high heat. Add the chicken in 2 batches and brown on each side, about 5 minutes per batch. Using a slotted spoon, transfer to a plate.

✦ Add the celery and garlic to the skillet and cook, stirring occasionally, until the celery is soft, about 4 minutes. Add the wine, bay leaves, salt and pepper, and bring to a boil. Cook for 2 minutes, then return the chicken to the skillet. Reduce the heat, stir in the

parsley and simmer, uncovered, until the liquid has evaporated and the chicken is cooked through, about 15 minutes. Remove the bay leaves and discard.

✦ Place on a warm serving platter and serve with fresh vegetables.

PER SERVING

177 calories/742 kilojoules; 28 g protein; 5.3 g fat, 26% of calories (1.4 g saturated, 7% of calories; 3.2 g monounsaturated, 16%; 0.7 g polyunsaturated, 3%); 0.3 g carbohydrate; 0.3 g dietary fiber; 241 mg sodium; 1 mg iron; 63 mg cholesterol.

*Chicken Cacciatore with
Black Olive and Anchovy Sauce*

Chicken with Lemons

POLLO AL LIMONI

Roast chicken is enjoyed in many different countries in a myriad of ways. This Italian version is flavored with a tangy marinade before roasting and makes a tasty change from ordinary roast chicken.

SERVES 6

1 chicken, about 3 lb (1.5 kg)
3 lemons, cut in half
3 garlic cloves, crushed
2 tablespoons finely chopped
   flat-leaf parsley
½ teaspoon red chili pepper
   flakes
½ teaspoon chili powder
¼ teaspoon salt
¼ teaspoon peppercorns,
   preferably a mixture of black,
   green and pink
thyme sprigs, for garnish

PREPARATION   *10 minutes plus*
                              1 hour marinating time

✦ Split the chicken down the backbone. Press down firmly with the palm of your hand to flatten. Place the chicken in a large dish.
✦ Squeeze the lemons into a bowl, reserving the lemon halves. Add the garlic, parsley, chili pepper flakes, chili powder, salt and peppercorns. Pour the lemon mixture on top of the chicken and place the lemon halves in the dish. Marinate in the refrigerator for 1 hour, turning several times.
✦ Preheat the oven to 400°F (200°C).

COOKING   *50 minutes*

✦ Transfer the chicken to a roasting pan. Pour the marinade on top and arrange the lemon halves around the sides. Roast until the juices run clear when the chicken is tested with a skewer in the thigh, about 45 minutes.
✦ Transfer to a serving dish, garnish with the thyme sprigs and serve with vegetables.

PER SERVING

226 calories/944 kilojoules; 25 g protein; 13 g fat, 52% of calories (4.5 g saturated, 18.2% of calories; 6.3 g monounsaturated, 25%; 2.2 g polyunsaturated, 8.8%); 1 g carbohydrate; 1.6 g dietary fiber; 139 mg sodium; 1.2 mg iron; 83 mg cholesterol.

Chicken Roman-Style

POLLO ALLA ROMANA

Since the days of the Roman Empire, two thousand years ago, Rome has had a reputation for fine food. Even the small *trattorie* serve their home-style meals with flair, and this dish is one of the favorites.

SERVES 4

1 large red bell pepper (capsicum)
1 large green bell pepper
   (capsicum)
1 tablespoon virgin olive oil
3 garlic cloves, finely chopped
8 boneless, skinless chicken
   thighs (thigh fillets), about
   2 oz (60 g) each
⅓ cup (3 fl oz/90 ml) dry
   white wine
1¾ cups (13 oz/410 g) canned
   plum (Roma) tomatoes
1 tablespoon shredded basil
1 tablespoon tomato paste
1 teaspoon dried oregano
½ teaspoon salt
¼ teaspoon freshly ground
   black pepper

PREPARATION   *10 minutes*

✦ Cut the bell peppers in half, remove the core and seeds and dice.

COOKING   *1 hour*

✦ Heat the oil in a large, non-stick skillet over medium-high heat. Add the garlic and cook, stirring, until golden, about 1 minute.
✦ Add the chicken and brown on both sides, in batches if necessary, about 5 minutes per batch. Stir in the wine, reduce the heat to low and simmer for 5 minutes. Stir in the remaining ingredients, cover and simmer for 30 minutes. Transfer the chicken to a serving

dish and keep warm. Simmer the sauce, uncovered, until the liquid is reduced, about 10 to 15 minutes.
✦ Place the chicken on a serving dish, pour the sauce on top and serve with pasta shells.

PER SERVING

242 calories/1013 kilojoules; 24 g protein; 11 g fat, 42% of calories (3.1 g saturated, 11.8% of calories; 6.3 g monounsaturated, 23.9%; 1.6 g polyunsaturated, 6.3%); 7 g carbohydrate; 2.2 g dietary fiber; 411 mg sodium; 2.3 mg iron; 162 mg cholesterol.

Chicken with Basil and Tomatoes

POLLO CON BASILICO E POMODORI

SERVES 4

1 lb (500 g) chicken breast fillets
1 tablespoon virgin olive oil
1 small onion, chopped
2 garlic cloves, crushed
1 lb (500 g) vine-ripened
   tomatoes, finely chopped
2 cups sliced mushrooms, about
   5 oz/150 g
½ cup (4 fl oz/125 ml) dry
   white wine
½ teaspoon salt
½ teaspoon freshly ground black
   pepper
1 cup shredded basil
basil sprigs, for garnish

Basil has been used in cooking for thousands of years—its name comes from the Ancient Greek for "the king of herbs." Italian cooks often partner it with tomato, and this delicious dish illustrates how well the flavors complement each other.

PREPARATION   *15 minutes*
✦ Cut the chicken into bite-sized pieces.

COOKING   *35 minutes*
✦ Heat the oil in a large, non-stick skillet over medium heat. Add the onion and garlic and cook, stirring continuously, until the onion is golden, about 5 minutes. Using a slotted spoon, transfer to a plate.
✦ Add the chicken to the skillet and cook, stirring, until lightly browned, about 5 minutes.
✦ Add the tomatoes, mushrooms, wine, salt and pepper. Return the onion and garlic to the skillet, stir well and bring to a boil. Reduce the heat and simmer until the liquid is reduced by half, about 15 minutes. Add the shredded basil and simmer for an additional 5 minutes.
✦ Place on a warm serving dish, garnish with the basil sprigs and serve with a pasta of your choice.

PER SERVING
232 calories/971 kilojoules; 32 g protein; 6.9 g fat, 26% of calories (1.7 g saturated, 6.5% of calories; 4.2 g monounsaturated, 15.9%; 1 g polyunsaturated, 3.6%); 5 g carbohydrate; 31 g dietary fiber; 335 mg sodium; 2.2 mg iron; 63 mg cholesterol.

Boats at Sestri Levante, a fishing port on the Italian Riviera.

Chicken with Basil and Tomatoes

Chicken Cacciatore

POLLO ALLA CACCIATORA

Although *pollo alla cacciatora* is regarded as a classic of Italian cuisine, there is no one definitive recipe. This one includes all the standard ingredients—tomatoes, onions, herbs and wine—and is a superb example of the Italian way of cooking chicken.

SERVES 4

2 tablespoons all-purpose
   (plain) flour
¼ teaspoon salt
¼ teaspoon freshly ground
   black pepper
8 boneless, skinless chicken
   thighs (thigh fillets), about
   2 oz (60 g) each
3 large, vine-ripened tomatoes,
   peeled and chopped
1 tablespoon virgin olive oil
1 carrot, finely chopped
1 small onion, finely chopped
1 garlic clove, finely chopped
1 bay leaf
¼ cup chopped flat-leaf parsley,
   plus extra for garnish
¼ cup (2 fl oz/60 ml) dry
   white wine

PREPARATION   *20 minutes*

✦ Combine the flour, salt and pepper in a clean, plastic bag. Add the chicken and toss to coat lightly. Shake off the excess flour.
✦ Place the tomatoes in a blender and purée.

COOKING   *55 minutes*

✦ Heat the oil in a large, non-stick skillet over medium-high heat. Add the chicken in 2 batches and cook until brown, about 5 minutes per batch. Using a slotted spoon, transfer the chicken to a plate.
✦ Add the carrot, onion and garlic to the skillet, lower the heat to medium, and cook, stirring continuously, until the carrot is tender, about 10 minutes.

✦ Stir in the tomatoes and bring to a boil. Stir in the bay leaf, parsley and wine. Return the chicken to the skillet, lower the heat and simmer until the chicken is cooked through, about 20 minutes. Remove the bay leaf and discard.
✦ Transfer to a serving dish, garnish with the extra chopped parsley and serve.

PER SERVING

244 calories/1020 kilojoules; 25 g protein; 11 g fat, 41% of calories (3.1 g saturated, 12% of calories; 6.3 g monounsaturated, 23%; 1.6 g polyunsaturated, 6%); 9 g carbohydrate; 2.9 g dietary fiber; 201 mg sodium; 2.2 mg iron; 163 mg cholesterol.

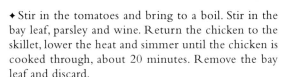
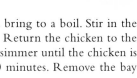

Chicken Breasts with Prosciutto and Cheese

PETTI DI POLLO CON PROSCIUTTO E PARMIGIANO

Parmesan, or *Parmigiano-Reggiano*, the best-known of Italian cheeses, has been a flavorsome specialty of Parma since the thirteenth century. Its crumbly consistency may make it hard to slice, but it doesn't matter if the slices are broken.

SERVES 6

2 tablespoons all-purpose
   (plain) flour
¼ teaspoon salt
¼ teaspoon freshly ground
   black pepper
6 chicken breasts, about 8 oz
   (250 g) each
2 tablespoons virgin olive oil
⅓ cup (3 fl oz/90 ml) Italian
   tomato sauce
6 thin slices Parmesan cheese
6 thin slices prosciutto

PREPARATION   *10 minutes*

✦ Combine the flour, salt and pepper on a plate. Coat the chicken pieces in the seasoned flour and shake off the excess flour.

COOKING   *25 minutes*

✦ Heat the oil in a large, non-stick skillet over medium-high heat. Add the chicken and cook, turning once, until cooked through, about 15 minutes.
✦ Preheat the broiler (grill).
✦ Place the chicken on a baking sheet. Spoon 1 scant tablespoon of the tomato sauce on top of each breast,

followed by a slice of the cheese and the prosciutto. Place under the broiler and broil until the cheese is warm and the prosciutto is crisp, about 5 minutes.
✦ Transfer to a serving platter and serve, accompanied by a salad.

PER SERVING

297 calories/1241 kilojoules; 39 g protein; 14 g fat, 41% of calories (5.7 g saturated, 17% of calories; 6.9 g monounsaturated, 20%; 1.4 g polyunsaturated, 4%); 4 g carbohydrate; 0.4 g dietary fiber; 116 mg sodium; 1.3 mg iron; 89 mg cholesterol.

*Chicken Breasts with
Prosciutto and Cheese*

Chicken Stuffed with Rice and Pine Nuts

DJAJ MAHSI

SERVES 6

¼ cup (about 1½ oz/45 g) rice
2 tablespoons (1 oz/30 g) margarine
7 oz (220 g) ground (minced) lamb loin (fillet)
1 large onion, finely chopped
2 tablespoons pine nuts
2 tablespoons raisins
½ teaspoon salt
¼ teaspoon freshly ground black pepper
1 chicken, about 3 lb (1.5 kg)
2 tablespoons plain yogurt
1 tablespoon honey

This imaginative way of combining fruit, poultry and lamb is typical of Middle Eastern cooking. The delicately flavored Italian or Mediterranean pine nuts have been used in the region for centuries.

PREPARATION   *55 minutes*

✦ Rinse the rice under cold running water.
✦ Bring a large saucepan of water to a boil. Add the rice and boil until cooked, about 25 minutes. Drain and set aside.
✦ Preheat the oven to 400°F (200°C).

COOKING   *1 hour and 10 minutes*

✦ Melt 1 tablespoon of the margarine in a large, non-stick skillet over medium-high heat. Add the lamb and cook, stirring continuously, until browned, about 3 minutes. Stir in the onion and cook until soft, about 3 minutes.
✦ Stir in the pine nuts and cook until lightly browned, about 3 minutes. Add the raisins, cooked rice, salt and pepper and stir to combine. Remove the skillet from the heat.
✦ Place the rice mixture in the cavity of the chicken. Wrap any extra stuffing in aluminum foil.

✦ Melt the remaining margarine in a small saucepan over low heat, then stir in the yogurt and honey. Brush half this mixture over the chicken.
✦ Place the chicken and the package of stuffing on a rack in a roasting pan and roast for 20 minutes.
✦ Brush the chicken with the remaining yogurt mixture. Lower the oven temperature to 350°F (180°C) and roast until the juices run clear when the chicken is tested with a skewer in the thigh, about 40 minutes. Cover the chicken with aluminum foil if it starts to brown too quickly.
✦ Place the chicken and extra stuffing on a serving platter. Serve with couscous.

PER SERVING

460 calories/1950 kilojoules; 38 g protein; 21 g fat, 40% of calories (6.3 g saturated, 12% of calories; 9.1 g monounsaturated, 17.2%; 5.6 g polyunsaturated, 10.8%); 33 g carbohydrate; 1 g dietary fiber; 311 mg sodium; 2.3 mg iron; 108 mg cholesterol.

Skewered Grilled Chicken with Garlic and Yogurt

SHISH DJAJ BI LABAN

SERVES 4

8 wooden skewers
½ cup (4 oz/125 g) plain yogurt
2 garlic cloves, crushed
1 teaspoon ground allspice
1 teaspoon sweet paprika
½ teaspoon hot paprika
½ teaspoon freshly ground black pepper
¼ teaspoon Tabasco sauce
1 lb (500 g) chicken breast fillets

Yogurt is used extensively in Middle Eastern cooking, and the making of yogurt is a regular activity in most households. In this recipe yogurt is mixed with both hot and sweet paprika, giving the chicken an appetizing red color.

PREPARATION *10 minutes plus 30 minutes soaking time*

✦ Soak the skewers in water for at least 30 minutes to prevent charring during cooking.
✦ Combine the yogurt, garlic, allspice, sweet and hot paprika, pepper and Tabasco sauce in a small bowl and stir to blend.
✦ Cut the chicken into bite-sized pieces and thread onto the skewers.
✦ Preheat the broiler (grill).

COOKING   *10 minutes*

✦ Brush one side of the chicken with the yogurt mixture. Place under the broiler and cook for 4 minutes.

Turn, brush the other side of the chicken with the mixture and broil until cooked through, about 4 minutes.
✦ Place the chicken on a serving platter and serve with a mixed green salad.

PER SERVING

169 calories/709 kilojoules; 30 g protein; 4.2 g fat, 23% of calories (1.8 g saturated, 9.9% of calories; 1.8 g monounsaturated, 9.9%; 0.6 g polyunsaturated, 3.2%); 2 g carbohydrate; 0.3 g dietary fiber; 92 mg sodium; 1 mg iron; 67 mg cholesterol.

Chicken Stuffed with Rice and Pine Nuts

Chicken with Lemon and Spices

DJAJ MTABBEL

MARINADE

¼ cup (2 fl oz/60 ml) freshly
   squeezed lemon or lime juice
1 tablespoon virgin olive oil
2 tablespoons chopped mint
1 tablespoon chopped flat-leaf
   parsley
2 teaspoons ground coriander
1½ teaspoons ground cumin
½ teaspoon ground turmeric

1 lb (500 g) chicken breast
   fillets, cut into strips
1 tablespoon virgin olive oil

Marinating chicken in lemon juice, spices and fresh herbs results in a light and flavorful dish. It is ideal for lunch, served with salad and hummus, the spread or dip made from puréed chickpeas, garlic, lemon juice and extra virgin olive oil.

PREPARATION   *10 minutes plus at least*
                              8 hours marinating time

✦ Combine the marinade ingredients in a large bowl. Add the chicken, stir to coat, cover, and marinate for at least 8 hours or overnight in the refrigerator.

COOKING   *10 minutes*

✦ Heat the oil in a medium-sized, non-stick skillet over medium-high heat. Add the chicken and cook until golden and cooked through, about 10 minutes.

✦ Stir in the remaining marinade, bring to a boil and cook for 2 minutes.
✦ Place the chicken and sauce in a serving dish and serve.

PER SERVING

209 calories/873 kilojoules; 29 g protein; 10 g fat, 43% of calories (2.1 g saturated, 9% of calories; 6.7 g monounsaturated, 28.8%; 1.2 g polyunsaturated, 5.2%); 1 g carbohydrate; 0.1 g dietary fiber; 72 mg sodium; 1.2 mg iron; 63 mg cholesterol.

Chicken with Olives

DJAJ MAH ZAITOUN

1 lemon, halved
4 chicken breasts, about 8 oz
   (250 g) each
1 cup (8 fl oz/250 ml) water
2 large onions, sliced
1 teaspoon sweet paprika
½ teaspoon ground ginger
¼ teaspoon freshly ground black
   pepper
½ cup (2½ oz/75 g) pitted
   black olives, sliced
parsley sprigs, for garnish

Olives have been enjoyed in the Middle East and the Mediterranean region since the days of the ancient Minoans and Phoenicians. This dish blends the salty, pungent flavor of juicy black olives with tangy lemon and spices.

PREPARATION   *10 minutes*

✦ Cut one half of the lemon into slices, and squeeze the juice from the other half.

COOKING   *45 minutes*

✦ Place the chicken skin side up in a saucepan just large enough to fit the pieces in a single layer.
✦ Pour the water into a large bowl and stir in the onions, paprika, ginger, pepper and lemon slices. Add to the saucepan with the chicken and bring to a boil over medium heat.
✦ Reduce the heat, cover and simmer for 20 minutes.
✦ Remove the lid and simmer until the juices run clear

when the chicken is tested with a skewer, an additional 15 minutes. Stir in the olives and simmer, stirring occasionally, for 5 minutes. Stir in the lemon juice.
✦ Transfer the chicken to a warm serving dish and spoon the sauce on top. Garnish with the parsley and serve with rice.

PER SERVING

246 calories/1028 kilojoules; 27 g protein; 14 g fat, 49% of calories (4.6 g saturated, 16.2% of calories; 6.9 g monounsaturated, 24%; 2.5 g polyunsaturated, 8.8%); 4 g carbohydrate; 2.2 g dietary fiber; 72 mg sodium; 1.3 mg iron; 76 mg cholesterol.

Chicken with Rice

DJAJ MAH RUZ

SERVES 4

½ cup (2 oz/60 g) plus
    1 tablespoon sliced almonds
1 lb (500 g) chicken breast fillets
1 cup (8 fl oz/250 ml) water
1 tablespoon virgin olive oil
1 onion, finely chopped
2 cups (16 fl oz/500 ml)
    chicken stock, skimmed of fat
1½ cups (10½ oz/330 g) long-
    grain rice
1 teaspoon ground cinnamon
1 teaspoon salt
½ cup (2½ oz/75 g) raisins

The people of the Middle East have been spice merchants for centuries and are experts in the creation of unique flavors. This layered dish subtly combines spices, fruit and nuts, to give the chicken and rice a distinctive taste and texture.

PREPARATION   *5 minutes*

◆ Toast the almonds in a dry, heavy-bottomed, non-stick skillet over medium heat, stirring continuously, until golden, about 1 to 2 minutes.

COOKING   *55 minutes*

◆ Place the chicken and water in a large saucepan and bring to a boil over medium heat. Reduce the heat and simmer for 10 minutes. Drain, reserving the liquid. Dice the chicken and keep warm.
◆ Wipe out the saucepan and add the oil. Heat over medium heat, then add the onion and cook until soft, about 3 minutes.
◆ Stir in the reserved cooking liquid and the chicken stock. Add the rice, ½ teaspoon of the cinnamon and the salt. Bring to a boil, then reduce the heat, cover and simmer until the rice is cooked and the liquid has almost evaporated, about 20 minutes. With a fork, stir in the ½ cup of almonds, the raisins and half of the diced chicken. Cook for an additional 5 minutes.

◆ Pile onto a warm serving dish. Top with the remaining chicken, and garnish with the remaining almonds and cinnamon. Serve with a salad.

PER SERVING
636 calories/2661 kilojoules; 39 g protein; 17 g fat, 24% of calories (2.6 g saturated, 4% of calories; 10.6 g monounsaturated, 15%; 3.8 g polyunsaturated, 5%); 82 g carbohydrate; 4.8 g dietary fiber; 751 mg sodium; 2.9 mg iron; 62 mg cholesterol.

Spicy Chicken with Chocolate, Chilies and Nuts

MOLE POBLANO DE POLLO

SERVES 6

5 teaspoons virgin olive oil
10 small red chilies, seeds
    removed and finely chopped
1 large onion, finely chopped
1 garlic clove, finely chopped
¼ cup ground almonds
¼ cup peanuts, finely chopped
1 tablespoon sesame seeds
¼ teaspoon anise seeds
¼ teaspoon ground cinnamon
¼ teaspoon ground coriander
¼ teaspoon black peppercorns
¾ cup (6 fl oz/180 ml) chicken
    stock, skimmed of fat
1 corn tortilla, lightly toasted
    and thinly sliced
½ cup chopped tomatillos
1 oz (30 g) bittersweet chocolate,
    chopped
1½ lb (750 g) chicken breast
    fillets
1 cup (8 fl oz/250 ml) water

Mole (pronounced "molay") is the Spanish word for sauce. This is one of the most famous of the Mexican *moles*, made with chilies and bittersweet chocolate. Chilies vary in their strength so adjust the quantity according to your taste.

PREPARATION *45 to 50 minutes plus 24 hours standing time*

✦ Heat 3 teaspoons of the oil in a small, non-stick skillet over medium-high heat. Add the chilies, onion and garlic and cook until the onion is soft, about 3 minutes.

✦ Reduce the heat to low and stir in the ground almonds, peanuts, sesame seeds, anise seeds, cinnamon, coriander, peppercorns. Cook, stirring occasionally, for about 5 minutes.

✦ Transfer the mixture to a food processor, add ¼ cup of the chicken stock and the tortilla and blend to a paste.

✦ Add the remaining oil and the tomatillos to the skillet and cook, stirring occasionally, for about 3 minutes. Add the tomatillos to the mixture in the food processor along with the remaining stock and process to blend.

✦ Transfer to a medium-sized saucepan and simmer, uncovered, for 30 minutes. Add the chocolate and stir until melted. Pour the sauce into a bowl, cool, cover and refrigerate for 24 hours.

COOKING *15 to 20 minutes*

✦ Place the chicken and water in a large saucepan over medium-high heat and bring to a boil. Reduce the heat and simmer until the chicken is cooked through, about 10 minutes. Drain, then return the chicken to the saucepan. Pour the sauce on top of the chicken and heat gently until hot.

✦ Transfer to a serving dish and serve with rice.

PER SERVING
309 calories/1294 kilojoules; 33 g protein; 16 g fat, 46% of calories (3.4 g saturated, 9.7% of calories; 9.1 g monounsaturated, 26.2%; 3.5 g polyunsaturated, 10.1%); 8 g carbohydrate; 2.4 g dietary fiber; 215 mg sodium; 1.8 mg iron; 63 mg cholesterol.

A street seller, with a range of produce, including chilies. These are a vital ingredient in Mexican cuisine.

Chicken Burritos

BURRITOS DE POLLO

GUACAMOLE

2 scallions (spring onions)
1 jalapeño chili, seeded
juice of 1 lime
1 ripe avocado
1 garlic clove, minced
½ teaspoon salt

3 cups (12 oz/375 g) cooked
  chicken
¼ head crisp lettuce
2 large, vine-ripened tomatoes,
  finely chopped
2 tablespoons fat-free French
  dressing
8 flour tortillas
1½ cups (12 oz/375 g) canned
  refried beans
1½ cups (4½ oz/140 g) freshly
  grated, sharp cheddar cheese
avocado slices, for garnish
parsley sprigs, for garnish

Refried beans *(frijoles refritos)* are an integral part of Mexican cuisine. Different varieties of beans are popular depending on the area. All are excellent sources of protein. Omitting guacamole will give a lower fat content.

PREPARATION   25 minutes

◆ Finely chop the scallions and the chili.
◆ To prepare the guacamole, place the scallions in a small bowl and marinate in the lime juice for 10 minutes. Mash the avocado in a small bowl and add to the scallions, along with the garlic, chili and salt. Stir to blend. Do not make ahead or the avocado will discolor.
◆ Shred the chicken and lettuce. Combine the lettuce and tomatoes in a medium-sized bowl and pour the French dressing on top.

COOKING   15 minutes

◆ Cook the tortillas in a dry, non-stick skillet over medium heat until lightly spotted with brown, but still soft, about 30 seconds each side. Remove to a plate and cover with a kitchen cloth to keep warm.
◆ Warm the refried beans in a small saucepan, stirring continuously.
◆ Spread each tortilla with an eighth each of the beans, chicken, cheese, guacamole and lettuce and tomatoes. Roll up, place on a serving platter and serve immediately, garnished with the avocado and parsley.

PER SERVING

355 calories/1485 kilojoules; 22 g protein; 21 g fat, 53% of calories (8 g saturated, 20.1% of calories; 9.8 g monounsaturated, 24.9%; 3.2 g polyunsaturated, 8%); 20 g carbohydrate; 4.3 g dietary fiber; 700 mg sodium; 1.3 mg iron; 77 mg cholesterol.

Stewed Chicken

GUISADO DE POLLO

6 chicken pieces, about 3 lb
  (1.5 kg)
½ cup (2½ oz/75 g) toasted
  almonds
½ cup coarsely chopped parsley
1 onion
2 garlic cloves
4 oz (125 g) chorizo sausage
1¾ cups (13 oz/410 g)
  chopped, canned tomatoes
  with their juice
1 tablespoon virgin olive oil
4 oz (125 g) ham steak, diced
2 teaspoons chopped rosemary
2 tablespoons dry sherry

This rich chicken dish, with the added spiciness of chorizo sausage, is a great meal in winter. Chorizo is a hot sausage available at speciality food stores. Mexican chorizo contains fresh pork, while in the Spanish version the pork is smoked.

PREPARATION   20 minutes

◆ Remove the skin from the chicken pieces.
◆ Combine the almonds, parsley, onion and garlic in a blender and finely chop.
◆ Remove the casing from the chorizo and thinly slice.
◆ Preheat the oven to 350°F (180°C).
◆ Drain the tomatoes, reserving the juice.

COOKING   55 minutes

◆ Heat the oil in a large, non-stick skillet over medium-high heat. Add the chicken and cook until golden, about 5 minutes per side. Using a slotted spoon, transfer the chicken to a casserole dish.
◆ Add the ham and chorizo to the skillet and cook, stirring continuously, until the chorizo is crisp, about 3 minutes. Add the tomatoes, rosemary and the almond mixture and cook for 5 minutes. Stir in the sherry and reserved tomato juice. Cook for 5 minutes.
◆ Pour the mixture over the chicken, cover and bake until the juices run clear when the chicken is tested with a skewer, about 30 minutes.
◆ Serve with a medley of fresh vegetables.

PER SERVING

360 calories/1507 kilojoules; 39 g protein; 20 g fat, 49% of calories (4.8 g saturated, 11.8% of calories; 11.6 g monounsaturated, 28.4%; 3.6 g polyunsaturated, 8.8%); 5 g carbohydrate; 3.1 g dietary fiber; 606 mg sodium; 3.2 mg iron; 103 mg cholesterol.

Chicken Burritos

Chicken with Vinegar

POLLO EN ADOBO

SERVES 8

1 chicken, about 4 lb (2 kg)
1½ cups (8 oz/250 g) peeled
   and chopped vine-ripened
   tomatoes
1–2 tablespoons chili powder
1 garlic clove
½ teaspoon ground cinnamon
½ teaspoon ground cumin
½ teaspoon dried oregano
½ teaspoon dried thyme
⅛ teaspoon ground clove
1 tablespoon virgin olive oil
1 onion, finely chopped
3 tablespoons cider vinegar

Dishes described as *adobo* contain dried chilies (or, for convenience, chili powder) and vinegar, a combination often used in marinades. Here the chili powder and vinegar are cooked in with the chicken. If desired, more chili powder can be used.

PREPARATION   *20 minutes*
◆ Using poultry shears, cut the chicken into 8 pieces.
◆ Combine the chili powder, garlic, cinnamon, oregano, thyme, cumin, cloves and tomatoes in a blender and purée.
◆ Preheat the oven to 350°F (180°C).

COOKING   *1 hour and 5 minutes*
◆ Heat the oil in a large, non-stick skillet over medium-high heat. Add the chicken in 2 batches, and brown all over, about 5 minutes per batch. Using a slotted spoon, transfer to a casserole dish.
◆ Add the onion to the skillet and cook until golden, about 3 minutes. Add the vinegar and cook, stirring continuously, for 1 minute. Stir in the tomato purée and simmer, stirring occasionally, for 5 minutes.

◆ Pour the sauce over the chicken. Bake until tender and the juices run clear when the chicken is tested with a skewer, about 40 minutes.
◆ Serve with mashed sweet potatoes and other vegetables of your choice.

PER SERVING
222 calories/929 kilojoules; 23 g protein; 14 g fat, 56% of calories (4.4 g saturated, 17.9% of calories; 7.3 g monounsaturated, 29.1%; 2.3 g polyunsaturated, 9%); 1 g carbohydrate; 0.6 g dietary fiber; 78 mg sodium; 1.2 mg iron; 77 mg cholesterol.

***Cooking tortillas
at a food stall;
a common sight
on Mexico's
bustling streets.***

Chicken with Vinegar

FROM MOROCCO

Chicken with Cumin and Paprika

DJEJ MECHOUI

SERVES 4

2 tablespoons (1 oz/30 g)
  unsalted butter, melted
1 small onion, quartered
1 garlic clove
1 tablespoon chopped cilantro
  (coriander)
1 tablespoon chopped flat-leaf
  parsley
1 teaspoon sweet paprika
1 teaspoon ground cumin
½ teaspoon salt
4 chicken breasts, about 8 oz
  (250 g) each

This recipe is from Marrakech, where it is renowned as a favorite dish of the Royal Court. Traditionally the chicken is cooked on a spit over hot coals, but is equally delicious when it is broiled or cooked on a barbecue.

PREPARATION   *10 minutes plus 1 hour standing time*
✦ Combine the melted butter, onion, garlic, cilantro, parsley, paprika, cumin and salt in a blender and blend to a paste. Carefully loosen the chicken skin without detaching it, then rub the paste under the chicken skin, cover and refrigerate for 1 hour.
✦ Preheat the broiler (grill).

COOKING   *40 minutes*
✦ Broil the chicken, turning frequently to avoid burning, until it is cooked through and the juices run clear when the chicken is tested with a skewer, about 25 minutes.

✦ Place the chicken on a serving platter and serve with couscous and a tossed salad.

PER SERVING

276 calories/1157 kilojoules; 26 g protein; 19 g fat, 51% of calories (8.2 g saturated, 26% of calories; 8.3 g monounsaturated, 27%; 2.5 g polyunsaturated, 8%); 1 g carbohydrate; 0.5 g dietary fiber; 315 mg sodium; 1.1 mg iron; 94 mg cholesterol.

Chicken with Sweet Tomato Jelly

DJEJ MATISHA MESLA

SERVES 6

1 tablespoon virgin olive oil
2 garlic cloves, finely chopped
pinch saffron threads
¼ teaspoon ground ginger
¼ teaspoon freshly ground black
  pepper
6 chicken pieces, about 3 lb (1.5 kg)
3 cups (1 lb/500 g) peeled and
  chopped vine-ripened tomatoes
1 onion, grated
2 tablespoons shredded cilantro
  (coriander)
1 teaspoon ground cinnamon
1 tablespoon tomato paste
2 tablespoons honey
1 tablespoon sesame seeds
cilantro (coriander) leaves,
  for garnish

In this savory dish, the tomatoes are simmered slowly, then the liquid is reduced quickly before honey is added. This brings out the flavor of the tomatoes and results in a sweet tomato "jelly" that is served as a sauce over the chicken.

PREPARATION   *20 minutes plus at least*
                     8 hours marinating time
✦ Mix together the oil, garlic, saffron, ginger and pepper in a small bowl, then rub the mixture over the chicken. Cover and refrigerate for at least 8 hours or preferably overnight.

COOKING   *1 hour and 5 minutes*
✦ Place the chicken and any marinating liquid in a large saucepan over medium-high heat. Stir in the tomatoes, onion, shredded cilantro and cinnamon. Bring to a boil, cover, reduce the heat and simmer for 40 minutes. Using a slotted spoon, transfer the chicken to a warm serving dish.

✦ Stir the tomato paste into the sauce in the saucepan. Increase the heat to medium-high and boil to reduce the sauce by half, stirring occasionally, about 10 minutes. Stir in the honey and sesame seeds, lower the heat and simmer for an additional 5 minutes.
✦ Pour the sauce on top of the chicken. Garnish with the cilantro leaves and serve with couscous or rice.

PER SERVING

284 calories/1187 kilojoules; 26 g protein; 16 g fat, 51% of calories (4.8 g saturated, 15% of calories; 8.4 g monounsaturated, 27%; 2.8 g polyunsaturated, 9%); 8 g carbohydrate; 1.6 g dietary fiber; 92 mg sodium; 1.6 mg iron; 83 mg cholesterol.

Chicken with Sweet Tomato Jelly

Couscous with Chicken and Vegetables

SESKU BIDAOUI

Couscous is tiny pasta made from semolina. The mark of a successful couscous dish is that each grain is light and fluffy. Producing classic couscous is time-consuming, and today packaged precooked couscous is often used.

SERVES 4

1½ cups (1 lb / 500 g) peeled
    and chopped vine-ripened
    tomatoes
2 turnips, about 8 oz (250 g)
3 oz (90 g) sugar snap peas
1 tablespoon (½ oz / 15 g)
    unsalted butter
1 large red onion, sliced
1 small red chili, seeded and
    finely chopped
1 teaspoon salt
¼ teaspoon freshly ground black
    pepper
pinch saffron threads
8 chicken drumsticks, about
    2½ oz (75 g) each
1 cinnamon stick
1 bouquet garni
6 pearl (pickling) onions
1 cup (8 fl oz / 250 ml) water
1¼ cups (about 7 oz / 220 g)
    sliced zucchini (courgettes)
¼ cup (2 fl oz / 60 ml) light
    cream
herb sprigs, for garnish

COUSCOUS

1 cup (8 fl oz / 250 ml) water
2 teaspoons virgin olive oil
1 teaspoon salt
1 cup (6½ oz / 200 g) precooked
    couscous
1 tablespoon (½ oz / 15 g)
    unsalted butter

PREPARATION   *25 minutes*

◆ Place half of the tomatoes in a blender and purée.
◆ Peel the turnips and cut into 1 in (2.5 cm) cubes.
◆ Trim the sugar snap peas.

COOKING   *1 hour*

◆ Melt the butter in a large, non-stick skillet over medium-high heat. Add the remaining chopped tomatoes, the red onion, chili, salt, pepper and saffron. Stir and cook for 1 minute. Add the chicken and cinnamon, reduce the heat and simmer for 15 minutes, turning the chicken after 7 minutes.
◆ Transfer the chicken and sauce to a large saucepan. Add the bouquet garni, turnip, pearl onions and water, cover, bring to a boil over low heat and simmer for 25 minutes.
◆ Add the zucchini and peas and cook, uncovered, for an additional 15 minutes. Remove the saucepan from the heat and discard the bouquet garni. Gently stir in the cream.

◆ Meanwhile, make the couscous. Bring the water, oil and salt to a boil in a medium-sized saucepan. Remove the saucepan from the heat and stir in the couscous. Let stand until the grains swell, about 2 minutes. Add the butter and heat over very low heat, stirring with a fork to separate the grains, until the butter melts, about 3 minutes.
◆ Pile the couscous onto a serving platter. Arrange the chicken and vegetables on top and pour over half of the sauce.
◆ Garnish with the herb sprigs and serve with the remaining sauce in a sauceboat on the side.

PER SERVING
*528 calories / 2209 kilojoules; 34 g protein; 28 g fat,
47% of calories (12.3 g saturated, 20.7% of calories;
12.3 g monounsaturated, 20.7%; 3.4 g polyunsaturated, 5.6%);
36 g carbohydrate; 6.5 g dietary fiber; 1301 mg sodium;
5.6 mg iron; 158 mg cholesterol.*

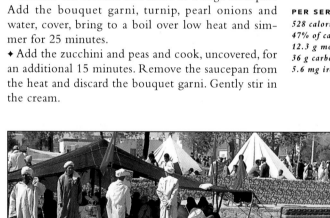

Pomp and ceremony on Throne Day in Morocco.

Couscous with Chicken and Vegetables

Chicken Tagine with Lemons

DJEJ M'QUALLI

SERVES 6

2 tablespoons warm water
pinch of saffron threads
6 chicken pieces, about 3 lb (1.5 kg)
2 tablespoons virgin olive oil
2 teaspoons margarine or butter
1½ cups (12 fl oz/375 ml)
    chicken stock, skimmed of fat
1 small onion
2 teaspoons finely chopped garlic
1 teaspoon finely chopped ginger
1 teaspoon salt
8 large black olives
zest of 1 lemon, cut into
    julienne strips
1 lemon, thinly sliced, for
    garnish

The lifestyle and recipes of North Africa favor the one-pot cooking method, with smaller quantities of chicken and meat used compared to Western standards. *Tagines,* or stews, are often the result, making a little meat go a long way.

PREPARATION   *15 minutes*
◆ Place the water in a small bowl, add the saffron and soak for 10 minutes.
◆ Remove the skin from the chicken pieces.

COOKING   *1 hour*
◆ Place the chicken, oil, margarine, stock, onion, garlic, ginger and salt in a large saucepan, cover and bring to a boil over medium-high heat. Reduce the heat to low and cook, occasionally spooning the liquid over the chicken, until it is cooked through and the juices run clear when the chicken is tested with a skewer, about 40 to 45 minutes. Remove the onion and discard.

◆ Add the olives and lemon zest to the saucepan and simmer, uncovered, for an additional 5 minutes.
◆ Place the chicken in a deep serving dish, pour the cooking juices on top and garnish with the lemon slices. Serve with hot crusty bread or over a bed of couscous.

PER SERVING
219 calories/918 kilojoules; 29 g protein; 9 g fat, 44% of calories (2 g saturated, 9% of calories; 6 g monounsaturated, 28%; 1 g polyunsaturated, 7%); 1 g carbohydrate; 1 g dietary fiber; 641 mg sodium; 1 mg iron; 63 mg cholesterol.

Crispy Spiced Chicken

DJEJ MAHAMMER

SERVES 6

¼ cup (2 fl oz/60 ml) hot water
pinch saffron threads
2 garlic cloves, crushed
2 teaspoons hot paprika
½ teaspoon ground cumin
½ teaspoon salt
¼ teaspoon ground turmeric
1 chicken, about 3 lb (1.5 kg)
½ cup (4 fl oz/125 ml) water
¼ cup (2 oz/60 g) unsalted
    butter, melted
1 onion, grated
2 chicken livers
1 tablespoon finely chopped
    cilantro (coriander)
cilantro (coriander) leaves, for
    garnish

A specialty of Rabat, this dish is popular throughout Morocco. The chicken is first braised, then finished in a skillet to create a crispy skin. Alternatively, the cooked chicken can be placed under a hot broiler and broiled until crispy.

PREPARATION   *35 minutes*
◆ Place the hot water in a small bowl and mix in the saffron. Cool for 15 minutes, then stir in the garlic, paprika, cumin, salt and turmeric.
◆ Split the chicken down the backbone. Press down firmly with the palm of your hand to flatten.

COOKING   *1 hour and 5 minutes*
◆ Place the ½ cup of water, half of the melted butter, the onion, chicken livers and chopped cilantro in a large saucepan. Add the chicken and spoon the saffron mixture on top. Bring to a boil, then reduce the heat and simmer for 20 minutes.
◆ Using a slotted spoon, remove the chicken livers from the saucepan. Chop them very finely and return them to the saucepan and simmer until the chicken is cooked through, and the juices run clear when the chicken is tested with a skewer in the thigh, about 30 minutes.

◆ Using a slotted spoon, remove the chicken from the saucepan, and cut into serving portions. Heat the remaining butter in a large, non-stick skillet over medium-high heat. Add the chicken pieces, skin side down, and cook until the skin is crispy, about 5 minutes. Place the chicken in a deep, warm serving dish.
◆ Meanwhile, bring the sauce to a boil and stir continuously until it has thickened, about 5 minutes.
◆ Pour the sauce on top of the chicken. Serve, garnished with the cilantro leaves.

PER SERVING
319 calories/1336 kilojoules; 28 g protein; 23 g fat, 63% of calories (10.2 g saturated, 29% of calories; 9.7 g monounsaturated, 26%; 3.1 g polyunsaturated, 8%); 1 g carbohydrate; 0.4 g dietary fiber; 276 mg sodium; 2.5 mg iron; 159 mg cholesterol.

Chicken Tagine with Lemons

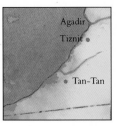

Chicken and Almond Pie

BISTEEYA

This delicious pie is synonymous with Morocco. Although it is classically made with a very fine pastry called *warkha,* phyllo is a good substitute. Traditionally the pie is made with whole pigeons or chicken, but this recipe uses boned chicken.

SERVES 8

TOPPING

¼ cup (3½ oz / 100 g) finely ground almonds
1 teaspoon confectioners' (icing) sugar
1 teaspoon ground cinnamon

3 garlic cloves, crushed
1 teaspoon salt
1½ lb (750 g) chicken breast fillets
3 tablespoons (1½ oz / 45 g) unsalted butter, melted
1 red onion, grated
2 teaspoons grated ginger
½ teaspoon freshly ground black pepper
½ cinnamon stick
¼ teaspoon ground turmeric
1 cup (8 fl oz / 250 ml) chicken stock, skimmed of fat
5 large eggs, lightly beaten
¼ cup (2 fl oz / 60 ml) freshly squeezed lemon juice
¼ cup finely chopped cilantro (coriander)
¼ cup finely chopped flat-leaf parsley
10 sheets phyllo pastry
grated zest of 1 lime

PREPARATION   *25 minutes plus 30 minutes standing time*

✦ Combine the topping ingredients in a small bowl. Mash the garlic and salt to a paste and rub over the chicken. Cover and refrigerate for 30 minutes, then rinse off the paste and dry the chicken.
✦ Brush a 10 in (25 cm) pie dish or a 9 × 12 × 2 in (24 × 28 × 5 cm) baking pan with some of the melted butter.

COOKING   *1¼ hours*

✦ Place the chicken, onion, ginger, pepper, cinnamon stick, turmeric and chicken stock in a large saucepan and bring to a boil. Reduce the heat and simmer for 15 minutes.
✦ Using a slotted spoon, transfer the chicken to a plate. Cool slightly, then shred.
✦ Meanwhile, increase the heat under the saucepan to medium and reduce the sauce by half, stirring occasionally, about 10 minutes. Remove the sauce from the heat, discard the cinnamon stick, and cool for 15 minutes.
✦ Preheat the oven to 400°F (200°C).

✦ Using a whisk, combine the eggs, lemon juice, cilantro and parsley in a small bowl. Stir into the sauce.
✦ Place 1 sheet of the phyllo in the baking pan, brushing it with a little of the melted butter and letting some of the pastry hang over the sides of the baking pan. Place another sheet on top and brush it with melted butter. Continue in this manner until there are 6 layers, then spread the shredded chicken over the pastry. Sprinkle the lime zest on top and pour over the egg mixture. Fold over the edges of the pastry. Butter the remaining sheets of the pastry as above and place on top of the pie, tucking the edges down the sides. Brush with the remaining butter and sprinkle with the topping.
✦ Bake until golden, about 30 minutes, then slice and serve.

PER SERVING
281 calories / 1177 kilojoules; 28 g protein; 14 g fat, 44% of calories (5.4 g saturated, 17% of calories; 6.4 g monounsaturated, 20%; 2.2 g polyunsaturated, 7%); 11 g carbohydrate; 1.2 g dietary fiber; 510 mg sodium; 1.7 mg iron; 174 mg cholesterol.

Sellers display their wares at Medina de Fes in Morocco.

Chicken and Almond Pie

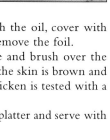

Chicken Stuffed with Sweetened Couscous

CHOUA

SERVES 6

1 cup (6½ oz/200 g) precooked
  couscous
1¼ cups (10 fl oz/300 ml)
  water
2 tablespoons (1 oz/30 g)
  margarine
2 tablespoons currants
1 tablespoon chopped blanched
  almonds
1 tablespoon chopped walnuts
1 tablespoon honey
¼ teaspoon ground cinnamon
¼ teaspoon ground cloves
¼ teaspoon ground cumin
¼ teaspoon ground ginger
¼ teaspoon ground turmeric
1 chicken, about 3 lb (1.5 kg)
1 teaspoon virgin olive oil

This dish is typical of North African cooking in that it shows the influence
of both the Middle East and the countries of southern Europe with a flavorful
mixture of nuts, fruit and spices.

PREPARATION   *15 minutes*
✦ Preheat the oven to 350°F (180°C).
✦ Place the precooked couscous in a large bowl. Bring
the water to a boil in a small saucepan, pour on top
of the couscous and let the grains swell for 2 minutes.
Stir in 1 tablespoon of the margarine, the currants, almonds, walnuts, honey and spices.
✦ Fill the cavity of the chicken with the couscous mixture and secure the opening with a skewer. Wrap any
extra stuffing in aluminum foil.

COOKING   *1 hour*
✦ Place the chicken, together with the package of extra stuffing, on a rack in a roasting pan. Fill the pan
with boiling water to come to ¾ in (1.5 cm) below
the rack. Brush the chicken with the oil, cover with
foil and bake for 40 minutes. Remove the foil.
✦ Melt the remaining margarine and brush over the
chicken. Cook uncovered, until the skin is brown and
the juices run clear when the chicken is tested with a
skewer, about 15 minutes.
✦ Place the chicken on a serving platter and serve with
the extra stuffing.

PER SERVING
*379 calories/1585 kilojoules; 28 g protein; 19 g fat,
44% of calories (5.6 g saturated, 12.8% of calories;
8.9 g monounsaturated, 20.6%; 4.5 g polyunsaturated, 10.6%);
26 g carbohydrate; 1.6 g dietary fiber; 111 mg sodium;
3.3 mg iron; 83 mg cholesterol.*

Chicken Stew with Prunes and Honey

DJEJ BIL BABCOCK

SERVES 6

⅓ cup (2 oz/60 g) blanched
  almonds
3 lb (1.5 kg) chicken thighs
1 cup (8 fl oz/250 ml) chicken
  stock, skimmed of fat
1 large onion, finely chopped
2 teaspoons margarine or butter
1 teaspoon sesame oil
½ teaspoon ground turmeric
1 teaspoon salt
½ teaspoon freshly ground black
  pepper
¾ cup (5 oz/155 g) pitted prunes
2 tablespoons honey
2 teaspoons ground cinnamon

In Morocco, chicken is usually reserved for special occasions and celebrations.
This dish is a delicious example of the way fruit and meat are combined in the
recipes of the region.

PREPARATION   *15 minutes*
✦ Toast the almonds in a small, dry skillet over me-
dium-high heat until golden, about 3 minutes.
✦ Remove the skin from the chicken

COOKING   *1 to 1¼ hours*
✦ Place the chicken pieces in a single layer in a large,
heavy-bottomed saucepan that has a tight-fitting lid.
Add the chicken stock, onion, margarine, oil, turmeric
salt and pepper. Cover and bring to a boil over medium-high heat.
✦ Reduce the heat to low. Cook, occasionally spooning the cooking liquid over the chicken, until the
juices run clear when tested with a skewer, about 40
to 45 minutes.
✦ Using a slotted spoon, remove the chicken pieces
from the saucepan and set aside.
✦ Stir in the prunes, honey and cinnamon. Simmer,
uncovered, until the sauce has reduced and thickened,
about 15 minutes.
✦ Return the chicken pieces to the saucepan and turn
to coat both sides with the sauce. Cook until they are
heated through.
✦ Transfer to a serving dish and garnish with the
toasted almonds. Serve with rice or crusty bread.

PER SERVING
*285 calories/1191 kilojoules; 24 g protein; 11 g fat, 38% of
calories (2 g saturated, 7% of calories; 6 g monounsaturated, 21%;
3 g polyunsaturated, 10%); 20 g carbohydrate; 3 g dietary fiber;
571 mg sodium; 2 mg iron; 71 mg cholesterol.*

Chicken Paprika

KURITSA S PAPRIKOY

SERVES 4

3 large, vine-ripened tomatoes
1 tablespoon (½ oz/15 g)
    margarine
1 large onion, chopped
2 tablespoons sweet paprika
1 small green bell pepper
    (capsicum), seeded and cut
    into strips
1 small red bell pepper
    (capsicum), seeded and cut
    into strips
8 boneless, skinless chicken
    thighs (thigh fillets), about
    2 oz (60 g) each
½ teaspoon dried marjoram
¼ teaspoon freshly ground black
    pepper
2 chicken boullion (stock) cubes,
    crumbled
1 cup (8 fl oz/250 ml) water
2 tablespoons light sour cream
chopped parsley, for garnish

This dish was brought to Russia by Hungarian immigrants. Sweet paprika (used here) is ground from the ripe flesh of the sweet red pepper. Hot paprika is made with the flesh and the seeds. For a richer flavor, make this dish a day in advance.

PREPARATION   *20 minutes*

◆ Place the tomatoes in a medium-sized bowl and cover with boiling water. Let stand until their skin starts to split, about 10 minutes, then remove from the water with a slotted spoon. Peel and coarsely chop the tomatoes.

COOKING   *40 minutes*

◆ Melt the margarine in a large saucepan over medium-high heat. Add the onion and cook until soft, about 3 minutes. Stir in the paprika and cook for 1 minute. Stir in the green and red bell peppers and cook for an additional 2 minutes.
◆ Add the chicken, tomatoes, marjoram, pepper, crumbled bouillon cubes and water and bring to a boil.

Reduce the heat and simmer until the chicken is tender and cooked through, about 30 minutes. Remove the saucepan from the heat.
◆ Mix 2 tablespoons of the cooking juices with the sour cream in a small bowl, then add to the chicken and stir through.
◆ Transfer to a serving dish and garnish with the chopped parsley. Serve with boiled rice.

PER SERVING
247 calories/1035 kilojoules; 25 g protein; 13 g fat, 46% of calories (4.5 g saturated, 16% of calories; 5.7 g monounsaturated, 20%; 2.8 g polyunsaturated, 10%); 7 g carbohydrate; 2.2 g dietary fiber; 585 mg sodium; 1.7 mg iron; 168 mg cholesterol.

Gaily clad young girls enjoying a snack on a Russian street.

Chicken with Okra

BAMIYOV

Okra is not often used in recipes from the West. It is neglected by many cooks because they have not been taught how to prepare and cook it well. One secret is to marinate the okra in vinegar first so that it doesn't become too glutinous.

SERVES 4

7 oz (220 g) okra
1 tablespoon white wine vinegar
¼ cup (2 fl oz / 60 ml) water
1¾ cups (13 oz / 410 g) coarsely chopped, canned tomatoes with their juice
2 tablespoons dry white wine
1 tablespoon freshly squeezed lemon juice
1 chicken bouillon (stock) cube, crumbled
½ teaspoon salt
¼ teaspoon freshly ground black pepper
2 tablespoons virgin olive oil
1 large onion, sliced
2 garlic cloves, finely chopped
8 mixed chicken pieces, about 2 lb (1 kg), removed skin
¼ cup chopped parsley
parsley sprigs, for garnish

PREPARATION   *15 minutes*
◆ Trim the stems off the okra, wash and pat dry. Place in a bowl and sprinkle with the vinegar. Let stand for 10 minutes, then drain.
◆ Pour the water into a medium-sized bowl. Add the tomatoes and their juice, wine, lemon juice, crumbled bouillon cube, salt and pepper.
◆ Preheat the oven to 350°F (180°C).

COOKING   *1 hour 10 minutes*
◆ Heat the oil in a large, non-stick skillet over medium-high heat. Add the onion and garlic and cook until the onion is soft, about 3 minutes. Transfer to a flameproof casserole dish.
◆ Add the chicken pieces to the skillet in 2 batches and brown, about 5 minutes per batch, then transfer to the casserole dish. Pour the tomato mixture on top. Cover.

◆ Bake for 40 minutes.
◆ Add the okra and bake, covered, until the juices run clear when the chicken is tested with a skewer, about 10 minutes. Using a slotted spoon, remove the chicken and keep warm. Place the casserole dish on the stove top and reduce the sauce, stirring continuously, over high heat, for 5 minutes. Stir in the chopped parsley. Return the chicken to the casserole dish and heat through.
◆ Place the chicken in a warm serving bowl and spoon the sauce on top. Garnish with the parsley sprigs and serve with rice.

PER SERVING
258 calories / 1081 kilojoules; 29 g protein; 13 g fat, 44% of calories (3.1 g saturated, 10% of calories; 8.4 g monounsaturated, 29%; 1.5 g polyunsaturated, 5%); 6 g carbohydrate; 3.9 g dietary fiber; 625 mg sodium; 2.5 mg iron; 98 mg cholesterol.

Chicken with Herbs and Tomatoes

CHAKHOKBILI

This dish comes from the former Russian province of Georgia, a small, rich agricultural area that lies to the east of the Black Sea. Many Georgians would use home-grown herbs and vegetables and a free-range chicken for this dish.

SERVES 4

2 onions
2 garlic cloves
2 tablespoons (1 oz / 30 g) margarine
1 lb (500 g) boneless, skinless chicken thighs (thigh fillets)
1¾ cup (13 oz / 410 g) canned tomatoes with their juice
2 tablespoons dry white wine
1½ tablespoons lemon juice
½ teaspoon salt
¼ teaspoon freshly ground black pepper
1 bay leaf
3 tablespoons chopped basil
3 tablespoons chopped cilantro (coriander) leaves
3 tablespoons chopped parsley
1 tablespoon chopped tarragon

PREPARATION   *10 minutes*
◆ Slice the onions and finely chop the garlic.

COOKING   *35 minutes*
◆ Melt the margarine in a large saucepan over medium heat. Add the onion and garlic and cook until the onion is soft, about 3 minutes.
◆ Add the chicken, tomatoes and their juice, wine, lemon juice, salt, pepper, bay leaf and half of each of the herbs. Cover, lower the heat and simmer for 20 minutes.

◆ Remove the lid from the saucepan and add the remaining herbs. Simmer, uncovered, for an additional 10 minutes. Remove the bay leaf.
◆ Transfer to a serving dish and serve with rice and lavash bread.

PER SERVING
254 calories / 1061 kilojoules; 24 g protein; 14 g fat, 48% of calories (4 g saturated, 13.9% of calories; 6.2 g monounsaturated, 21.1%; 3.8 g polyunsaturated, 13%); 7 g carbohydrate; 2.4 g dietary fiber; 456 mg sodium; 1.5 mg iron; 163 mg cholesterol.

Chicken with Okra

Marinated Azerbaijan Chicken

JUJA KABOB

SERVES 4

8 wooden skewers
¼ teaspoon saffron threads
1 tablespoon warm water
1 lb (500 g) chicken breast fillets
1 cup (8 oz / 250 g) plain yogurt
1 onion, finely chopped
2 garlic cloves, finely chopped
¼ cup finely chopped mint
½ teaspoon hot paprika
½ teaspoon sweet paprika
1 small red bell pepper
*   (capsicum)*

This dish comes from the former Russian province of Azerbaijan. Traditionally, these kebabs are eaten wrapped in paper-thin sheets of lavash bread, sold in many supermarkets. Marinate the kebabs overnight.

PREPARATION   *20 minutes plus marinating time*

◆ Soak the skewers in cold water for at least 30 minutes, to prevent charring.
◆ Soak the saffron threads in the warm water for 5 minutes, then strain the saffron, reserving the liquid.
◆ Cut the chicken into bite-sized pieces.
◆ Combine the yogurt, onion, garlic, saffron liquid, mint and the hot and sweet paprika in a small bowl.
◆ Dice the bell pepper into bite-sized pieces, large enough to thread on skewers.
◆ Thread the chicken and bell pepper pieces alternately onto the skewers and place in a shallow dish. Spoon the marinade on top of the kebabs. Cover and marinate overnight in the refrigerator.

COOKING   *10 minutes*

◆ Preheat the broiler (grill). Broil the kebabs, turning several times, until cooked through, about 10 minutes.
◆ Arrange on a serving platter and serve with rice.

PER SERVING
204 calories / 854 kilojoules; 33 g protein; 5.4 g fat, 24% of calories (2.7 g saturated, 12% of calories; 2.1 g monounsaturated, 9.4%; 0.6 g polyunsaturated, 2.6%); 5 g carbohydrate; 1 g dietary fiber; 116 mg sodium; 1.5 mg iron; 70 mg cholesterol.

Old-world charm and dignity are evident in a local store in the Kazan region.

Marinated Azerbaijan Chicken

Chicken with Mediterranean Summer Vegetables

POLLO A LA CATALANA CON VERDURAS

The combination of onions, peppers, eggplants and tomatoes is typical of Spanish cuisine, as well as the cooking of many of the Mediterranean countries. This dish is a traditional specialty of Spain's Catalan region.

SERVES 4

GARLIC TOAST

½ *baguette (French bread stick)*
1 *tablespoon extra virgin olive oil*
1 *teaspoon crushed garlic*

1 *tablespoon virgin olive oil*
2 *red onions, sliced*
2 *garlic cloves, finely chopped*
4 *oz (125 g) lean bacon*
8 *boneless, skinless chicken thighs (thigh fillets), about 2 oz (60 g) each*
1 *red bell pepper (capsicum), coarsely chopped*
1 *green bell pepper (capsicum), coarsely chopped*
3 *baby eggplants (aubergines), sliced*
1¾ *cups (13 oz/410 g) coarsley chopped, canned tomatoes, drained*
¼ *cup (2 fl oz/60 ml) white wine*
1 *bouquet garni*
1 *chicken bouillon (stock) cube, crumbled*
freshly ground black pepper

PREPARATION   *30 minutes*

✦ Slice the bread into 1 in (2.5 cm) slices for the garlic toast.
✦ Mix together the extra virgin olive oil and the crushed garlic in a small bowl.
✦ Preheat the oven to 350°F (180°C).

COOKING   *50 minutes*

✦ Heat the virgin olive oil in a large, non-stick skillet over medium-high heat. Add the onions, garlic and bacon. Cook, stirring continuously, until the onions are soft and golden, about 3 minutes. Using a slotted spoon, transfer to a large casserole dish.
✦ Add the chicken to the skillet and brown on both sides, about 5 minutes. Add to the casserole dish.
✦ Mix together the red and green bell peppers, egg-plants, tomatoes, wine, bouquet garni, crumbled bouillon cube and pepper in a medium-sized bowl. Pour this mixture on top of the chicken. Cover and bake until the chicken is tender and cooked through, about 30 minutes. Remove the bouquet garni and discard.
✦ Meanwhile, preheat the broiler (grill).
✦ Place the bread slices under the broiler and toast on one side. Remove from the broiler, and, using a pastry brush, brush the oil and garlic mixture over the untoasted side of each slice of bread. Broil until toasted. Serve with the chicken.

PER SERVING
433 calories/1814 kilojoules; 36 g protein; 18 g fat, 37% of calories (4.9 g saturated, 10% of calories; 10.3 g monounsaturated, 21%; 2.8 g polyunsaturated, 6%); 30 g carbohydrate; 4.9 g dietary fiber; 1045 mg sodium; 3.1 mg iron; 180 mg cholesterol.

Building archways is considered an art in Spain. Here a simple arch frames the countryside, creating a serene picture.

Chicken with Mediterranean Summer Vegetables

Braised Chicken with Almonds
POLLO EN PEPITORIA

If you visit Spain during spring you will see the spectacular almond trees in full bloom throughout the countryside. They are planted for more than their beautiful blossoms; the almond's delicate flavor is part of many Spanish dishes.

SERVES 4

2 large, hard-boiled eggs
1½ tablespoons all-purpose (plain) flour
½ teaspoon salt
¼ teaspoon freshly ground black pepper
8 skinless chicken drumsticks, about 4 oz (125 g) each
1 tablespoon virgin olive oil
2 onions, finely chopped
1 tablespoon chopped parsley
2 bay leaves
¾ cup (6 fl oz/180 ml) water
¼ cup (2 fl oz/60 ml) dry white wine
2 tablespoons finely ground almonds
½ teaspoon sweet paprika
2 garlic cloves, crushed
pinch crushed saffron threads
parsley leaves, for garnish

PREPARATION   *20 minutes*
◆ Shell the hard-boiled eggs and separate the whites from the yolks. Finely chop the egg whites and set aside both the egg whites and the yolks.
◆ Combine the flour, salt and pepper in a clean, plastic bag. Toss the chicken in the flour to coat lightly. Shake off the excess flour.

COOKING   *40 minutes*
◆ Heat the oil in a large, non-stick skillet over medium heat. Add the chicken and cook until golden all over, about 5 minutes. Using a slotted spoon, transfer to a large saucepan.
◆ Add the onions to the skillet and cook until soft, about 3 minutes, then transfer to the saucepan. Add the parsley, bay leaves, water and wine and stir well. Cook over medium heat, stirring occasionally, until the chicken is cooked through, about 20 minutes.

◆ Transfer the chicken to a serving dish and keep warm.
◆ In a small bowl, combine the ground almonds, paprika, egg yolks, garlic and saffron. Add a few tablespoons of the cooking liquid and stir to form a paste.
◆ Add the paste to the saucepan and bring to a boil over low heat. Simmer for 3 minutes. Remove the bay leaves.
◆ Pour the sauce over the chicken. Garnish with the chopped egg white and parsley leaves, and serve.

PER SERVING
301 calories/1262 kilojoules; 30 g protein; 17 g fat, 49% of calories (4.3 g saturated, 12.3% of calories; 9.7 g monounsaturated, 27.9%; 3 g polyunsaturated, 8.8%); 6 g carbohydrate; 1.8 g dietary fiber; 388 mg sodium; 3 mg iron; 206 mg cholesterol.

Chicken with Sweet Red Peppers and Tomatoes
POLLO CHILINDRON

This is a popular dish from Aragon, in the northeast of Spain, a region well known for the fine fruit and vegetables grown there. *Chilindrón* always refers to a rich sauce of tomatoes, peppers, garlic and onion.

SERVES 4

1 green bell pepper (capsicum)
1 red bell pepper (capsicum)
1 banana chili
1 small red chili
3 vine-ripened tomatoes
1 tablespoon virgin olive oil
1 lb (500 g) boneless, skinless chicken thighs (thigh fillets)
1 large red onion, sliced
2 garlic cloves, finely chopped
½ cup (4 fl oz/125 ml) dry white wine
1 chicken bouillon (stock) cube, crumbled
5 oz (150 g) lean ham, diced

PREPARATION   *15 minutes*
◆ Seed the bell peppers and chilies, and chop.
◆ Place the tomatoes in a bowl and cover with boiling water. Let stand until their skin begins to split, about 10 minutes. Using a slotted spoon, remove the tomatoes from the water and peel and chop them.

COOKING   *30 minutes*
◆ Heat the oil in a large, non-stick skillet over medium-high heat. Add the chicken, in batches, and brown on both sides, about 5 minutes per batch. Using a slotted spoon, transfer to a large saucepan.
◆ Add the onion, peppers, chilies, garlic and tomatoes to the skillet. Cook until the onion is soft, about 3

minutes, and then pour the mixture on top of the chicken. Add the wine, crumbled bouillon cube and ham and stir well. Cover and cook over medium heat until the chicken is tender and cooked through, about 15 minutes.
◆ Transfer to a serving dish and serve with boiled rice.

PER SERVING
290 calories/1213 kilojoules; 32 g protein; 13 g fat, 39% of calories (3.8 g saturated, 11% of calories; 7.6 g monounsaturated, 23%; 1.6 g polyunsaturated, 5%); 7 g carbohydrate; 2.7 g dietary fiber; 919 mg sodium; 2.6 mg iron; 182 mg cholesterol.

Braised Chicken with Almonds

Chicken with Rice

ARROZ CON POLLO

SERVES 4

1 teaspoon freshly ground black
   pepper
8 skinless chicken drumsticks,
   about 4 oz (125 g) each
2 tablespoons virgin olive oil
8 oz (250 g) bacon, finely
   chopped
1 onion, finely chopped
2 garlic cloves, finely chopped
1¾ cups (13 oz/410 g) coarsely
   chopped, canned tomatoes,
   drained
2 teaspoons sweet paprika
1¼ cups (10 fl oz/300 ml)
   water
1 cup (7 oz/220 g) long-grain
   rice
½ cup (2½ oz/85 g) peas
pinch crushed saffron threads
herbs, for garnish

Saffron threads are the delicate stamens of the crocus plant. This expensive spice gives a wonderful flavor, color and aroma to one of the most popular of all Spanish chicken dishes.

PREPARATION   *15 minutes*
◆ Sprinkle the pepper evenly over the chicken drumsticks.
◆ Preheat the oven to 350°F (180°C).

COOKING   *50 minutes*
◆ Heat the oil in a large, non-stick skillet over medium-high heat. Add the drumsticks and cook until golden all over, about 5 minutes. Using a slotted spoon, transfer them to a casserole dish.
◆ Add the bacon, onion and garlic to the skillet and cook until the onion is soft, about 3 minutes. Add the tomatoes and paprika and cook until all the liquid has evaporated, about 5 minutes. Transfer the mixture to the casserole dish.

◆ Bring the water to a boil, then add to the casserole dish together with the rice, peas and saffron. Stir well. Cover and bake until the juices run clear when the chicken is tested with a skewer and the rice is tender, about 30 minutes.
◆ Garnish with the herbs and serve, accompanied by a salad if desired.

PER SERVING
*540 calories/2259 kilojoules; 43 g protein; 18 g fat,
30% of calories (4.9 g saturated, 8.1% of calories;
10.6 g monounsaturated, 17.7%; 2.5 g polyunsaturated, 4.2%);
50 g carbohydrate; 4.4 g dietary fiber; 1112 mg sodium;
3.9 mg iron; 139 mg cholesterol.*

*One of Madrid's
many cafeterías;
these eating places
specialize in tasty
quick food for busy
city-dwellers.*

Chicken with Rice

Chicken Asturian-Style

POLLO ASTURIANA

3 lb (1.5 kg) chicken thighs
3 tablespoons all-purpose
  (plain) flour
½ teaspoon sweet paprika
½ teaspoon salt
½ teaspoon freshly ground black
  pepper
2 tablespoons virgin olive oil
1 onion, chopped
1 green cooking apple, peeled
  and chopped
½ cup (4 oz/125 g) diced ham
2 teaspoons crushed garlic
1 cup (8 fl oz/250 ml) hard
  (dry) apple cider
6 raw jumbo (large) shrimp
  (prawns), shelled and deveined
1 tablespoon chopped flat-leaf
  parsley
1 cup garlic croutons
apple slices, for garnish
flat-leaf parsley sprigs, for
  garnish

Asturias is famous for its frothy amber-colored apple cider with a sour tang.
Some of the recipes of this region of northern Spain are very similar to those
of France's Normandy and Brittany.

PREPARATION   *20 minutes*
✦ Remove the skin from the chicken.
✦ Combine the flour, paprika, salt and pepper in a
clean, plastic bag. Add the chicken and toss to coat
lightly. Shake to remove the excess flour.

COOKING   *50 minutes*
✦ Heat the oil in a large skillet over medium-high heat.
Add the chicken in 2 batches and cook until browned
on both sides, about 5 minutes per batch. Using a slotted spoon, transfer the chicken to a plate and set aside.
Discard all but 2 teaspoons of the oil.
✦ Reduce the heat to low. Add the onion, apple, ham
and garlic and cook until the onion is soft, about 3
minutes. Add the cider, return the chicken to the skillet and simmer gently until cooked through, about 20
minutes.

✦ Add the shrimp and parsley. Simmer until the shrimp
are just cooked through, about 5 minutes.
✦ Transfer to a serving dish and garnish with the
croutons, apple slices and parsley sprigs. Serve with a
green vegetable and rice.

PER SERVING
*286 calories/1196 kilojoules; 30 g protein; 9 g fat, 35% of
calories (2 g saturated, 9% of calories; 6 g monounsaturated, 22%;
1 g polyunsaturated, 4%); 16 g carbohydrate; 1 g dietary fiber;
625 mg sodium; 2 mg iron; 110 mg cholesterol.*

Farmhouse Chicken

CALDILLO DE POLLO

1 tablespoon virgin olive oil
½ red onion, very finely chopped
2 garlic cloves, very finely
  chopped
½ teaspoon salt
¼ teaspoon freshly ground black
  pepper
1 chicken, about 3 lb (1.5 kg)

SAUCE
pinch saffron threads
1 teaspoon hot water
2 large, hard-boiled eggs
1 garlic clove, chopped
2 tablespoons water
1 tablespoon white wine vinegar
¼ cup (2 fl oz/60 ml) extra
  virgin olive oil

This dish comes from the province of Cordoba, a predominantly rural area. The
sauce is rather like a mayonnaise in that it may separate if it is heated. It is also
quite high in fat. Present it separately from the chicken and use as desired.

PREPARATION   *20 minutes*
✦ Preheat the oven to 375°F (190°C).
✦ Combine the virgin olive oil, onion, garlic, salt and
pepper in a bowl. Rub the mixture all over the
chicken.
✦ For the sauce, soak the saffron threads in the hot
water.
✦ Separate the egg yolks from the egg whites, and chop
the whites coarsely.

COOKING   *1 hour and 15 minutes*
✦ Place the chicken on a rack in a roasting pan and
roast, basting occasionally with the pan juices, until the
juices run clear when the chicken is tested with a
skewer, about 1 hour.

✦ During the final 30 minutes of roasting, make the
sauce. Combine the egg yolks, saffron and its liquid,
garlic, water and vinegar in a food processor. With the
processor on low, very slowly trickle in the extra virgin olive oil until the sauce has emulsified. Pour into
a medium-sized serving bowl and stir in the egg white.
✦ Carve the chicken and place on a warm serving platter. Serve the sauce on the side.

PER SERVING (INCLUDES SAUCE)
*346 calories/1447 kilojoules; 27 g protein; 26 g fat, 68% of
calories (6.7 g saturated, 18% of calories; 15.8 g monounsaturated,
41%; 3.5 g polyunsaturated, 9%); 0.6 g carbohydrate; 0.4 g dietary
fiber; 254 mg sodium; 1.3 mg iron; 152 mg cholesterol.*

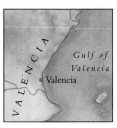

Valencian Rice with Chicken and Seafood

PAELLA A LA VALENCIANA

SERVES 6

2 lb (1 kg) chicken pieces

1 teaspoon sweet paprika

2 tablespoons virgin olive oil

8 oz (250 g) lean bacon, chopped

1 red onion, chopped

2 garlic cloves

1 teaspoon salt

1 teaspoon freshly ground black pepper

2 tablespoons tomato paste

2 cups (14 oz / 440 g) long-grain rice

¼ teaspoon saffron threads or ground saffron

3 cups (24 fl oz / 750 ml) chicken stock, skimmed of fat

1 cup (4 oz / 125 g) baby peas

1 small red bell pepper (capsicum), diced

12 raw jumbo (large) shrimp (prawns), shelled and deveined

1 tablespoon dry sherry, optional

Throughout Spain there are hundreds of authentic paella recipes, for this is a colorful rice dish into which just about anything can go. Usually it contains chicken, meat and seafood. This is an easy version of the traditional favorite.

PREPARATION   *15 minutes*

◆ Remove the skin from the chicken. Chop each chicken piece into 2 or 3 pieces and sprinkle with the paprika.

COOKING   *1 hour*

◆ Heat the oil in a large, heavy-bottomed skillet over medium heat. Add the chicken and cook, stirring occasionally, until well browned on all sides, about 10 minutes. Transfer to a plate and set aside.

◆ Add the bacon to the skillet and cook, stirring occasionally, for 4 minutes, then transfer to the plate with the chicken. Add the onion, garlic, salt and pepper to the skillet and cook, stirring, for 2 minutes. Add the tomato paste and rice and cook, stirring, for 2 minutes. Add the saffron, stock and peas, return the chicken and bacon to the skillet and stir well. Cover, reduce the heat to very low and cook for 15 minutes.

◆ Add the bell pepper, shrimp and sherry, if using, to the skillet without stirring. Cover and cook until the rice is tender and the stock has been absorbed, about 20 minutes. Remove from the heat and let stand with the lid on for 5 minutes.

◆ Place in a serving dish and serve with warm crusty bread and salad.

PER SERVING

462 calories / 1935 kilojoules; 39 g protein; 9 g fat, 25% of calories (3 g saturated, 6% of calories; 7 g monounsaturated, 16%; 1 g polyunsaturated, 3%); 46 g carbohydrate; 3 g dietary fiber; 1191 mg sodium; 2 mg iron; 138 mg cholesterol.

A band adds a musical note to a Spanish street parade.

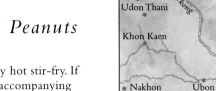

Stir-Fried Chicken with Chilies and Peanuts

GAI PAHT PRIK HAENG

The whole peanuts add crunch and textural contrast to this spicy hot stir-fry. If you prefer a milder taste, remove the seeds from the chilies. An accompanying serving of rice will help absorb some of the chili's heat.

SERVES 4

*3 oz (100 g) snow peas
  (mange-tout)*
1 tablespoon vegetable oil
2 garlic cloves, finely chopped
4 small red chilies, thinly sliced
*1 lb (500 g) boneless, skinless
  chicken thighs (thigh fillets),
  thinly sliced*
*⅓ cup (2 oz/60 g) roasted
  unsalted peanuts*
*¼ cup (2 fl oz/60ml) chicken
  stock, skimmed of fat*
2 tablespoons soy sauce
1 tablespoon fish sauce
¼ teaspoon sugar

PREPARATION   *15 minutes*
✦ Wash the snow peas and trim them.

COOKING   *15 minutes*
✦ Heat the oil in a wok or large, heavy-bottomed skillet over medium-high heat. Add the garlic and stir-fry until golden, about 1 minute. Add the chilies and stir-fry for 30 seconds. Using a slotted spoon, remove the garlic and chilies and set aside.
✦ Add the chicken, in 2 batches, and cook until light golden and tender, about 3 minutes per batch.
✦ Return all the chicken, the garlic and chilies to the wok and stir in the remaining ingredients. Cook for 2 minutes.

✦ Transfer to a serving dish and serve immediately with boiled rice.

PER SERVING
*302 calories/1264 kilojoules; 28 g protein; 19 g fat,
55% of calories (4.4 g saturated, 12.7% of calories;
9.5 g monounsaturated, 27.5%; 5.1 g polyunsaturated, 14.8%);
6 g carbohydrate; 2.5 g dietary fiber; 662 mg sodium; 2.2 mg iron;
162 mg cholesterol.*

A village nestles at the edge of this fertile river valley in Thailand.

Chiang Mai Curried Noodles

KHAO SOI

SERVES 4

2 garlic cloves
1 tablespoon vegetable oil
1 teaspoon red curry paste
½ cup (4 fl oz/125 ml) coconut
  milk
1 lb (500 g) ground (minced)
  chicken
1 cup (8 fl oz/250 ml) water
2 tablespoons fish sauce
1 teaspoon freshly squeezed
  lemon juice
1 teaspoon curry powder
½ teaspoon ground turmeric
½ teaspoon sugar
8 oz (250 g) fresh egg noodles
cilantro (coriander) leaves, for
  garnish

This popular dish is named after the city of Chiang Mai in the north of Thailand, capital of the old La Na Tha kingdom. Fresh egg noodles can be found in specialty Asian food stores.

PREPARATION   7 minutes
✦ Finely chop the garlic.

COOKING   15 minutes
✦ Heat the oil in a wok over medium-high heat. Add the garlic and cook, stirring, until golden, about 1 minute.
✦ Stir in the curry paste and cook, stirring, for 1 minute.
✦ Add the coconut milk and cook, stirring until thickened, about 2 to 3 minutes.
✦ Add the chicken and cook, stirring and breaking up any lumps, until cooked through, about 5 minutes.

Add the water, fish sauce, lemon juice, curry powder, turmeric and sugar. Cook for 5 minutes.
✦ Stir in the noodles and cook for 1 minute.
✦ Place in a warm serving dish, garnish with the cilantro leaves and serve immediately.

PER SERVING
478 calories/2002 kilojoules; 36 g protein; 15 g fat, 30% of calories (6.7 g saturated, 13 % of calories; 4.9 g monounsaturated, 10%; 3.4 g polyunsaturated, 7%); 48 g carbohydrate; 1.9 g dietary fiber; 233 mg sodium; 3.1 mg iron; 98 mg cholesterol.

Chicken in Red Curry Sauce

GAENG PET GAI

SERVES 4

1 cup (8 fl oz/250 ml) coconut
  milk
1 tablespoon vegetable oil
2 garlic cloves, finely chopped
1 tablespoon red curry paste
1½ tablespoons fish sauce
½ teaspoon sugar
1 lb (500 g) boneless, skinless
  chicken thighs (thigh fillets),
  thinly sliced
¼ cup (2 fl oz/60 ml) water
3 kaffir lime or lime leaves,
  shredded
⅔ cup (4 oz/125 g) canned
  sliced bamboo shoots
¼ cup shredded purple basil
purple basil leaves, for garnish

Canned red curry paste can be purchased in specialty Asian stores and some large supermarkets. Purple basil, which has a purple stem and green leaves, has a distinctive aniseed flavor. It can be replaced by regular basil if necessary.

PREPARATION   20 minutes
✦ Warm the coconut milk in a microwave oven until it is tepid, about 1 minute, or heat in a small saucepan over low heat for about 1 minute.

COOKING   25 minutes
✦ Heat the oil in a wok over medium-high heat. Add the garlic and cook, stirring, until golden, about 1 minute. Add the curry paste and cook, stirring continuously, for 1 minute.
✦ Add the warm coconut milk. Cook until thickened, about 2 to 3 minutes.
✦ Stir in the fish sauce and sugar.

✦ Add the chicken and cook until tender, about 10 to 15 minutes. Add the water and simmer for 1 minute.
✦ Stir in the kaffir lime leaves, bamboo shoots and shredded basil. Cook for 1 minute.
✦ Transfer to a serving dish and serve with boiled rice, garnished with the basil leaves.

PER SERVING
311 calories/1303 kilojoules; 25 g protein; 21 g fat, 59% of calories (11.4 g saturated, 31.9% of calories; 6 g monounsaturated, 17.1%; 3.6 g polyunsaturated, 10%); 7 g carbohydrate; 0.8 g dietary fiber; 196 mg sodium; 2 mg iron; 163 mg cholesterol.

Chicken in Red Curry Sauce

Curried Chicken with Lemongrass

OOK GAI

SERVES 4

CURRY PASTE

*1 stalk lemongrass, trimmed
    and chopped*
1 in (2.5 cm) galangal
*2 kaffir lime or lime leaves,
    thinly sliced*
*3 shallots (French shallots),
    chopped*
4 cilantro (coriander) roots, chopped
2 garlic cloves
4 small red chilies
1 teaspoon shrimp paste
1 teaspoon ground turmeric

*2 small, well-shaped red chilies,
    for chili flowers*
1 tablespoon vegetable oil
1 garlic clove, finely chopped
*1 lb (500 g) boneless, skinless
    chicken thighs (thigh fillets),
    sliced*
2 tablespoons fish sauce
*¾ cup (6 fl oz / 180 ml) chicken
    stock, skimmed of fat*
½ teaspoon sugar
*1 stalk lemongrass, trimmed
    and finely sliced*
*6 kaffir lime or lime leaves,
    shredded*
lime slices, for garnish

Although the curry paste is a bit time-consuming to make, it is well worth the effort. You will only need about half the quantity for this recipe—the leftover paste can be frozen for another use. Shrimp paste is available from specialty Asian food stores.

PREPARATION *10 minutes plus 30 minutes standing time*
✦ Combine the curry paste ingredients in a blender, or use a mortar and pestle, and blend or pound until smooth.
✦ Use a very sharp knife to make 2 or 3 cuts from the pointed end of each chili almost to the base of the stem end. Place in a bowl of iced water until the "petals" curl, at least 30 minutes.

COOKING *20 minutes*
✦ Heat the oil in a wok over medium-high heat. Add the garlic and cook, stirring continuously, until golden, about 1 minute.
✦ Add 1½ tablespoons of the curry paste, reserving the rest of the paste for future use, and cook, stirring, for 30 seconds.

✦ Add the chicken, fish sauce, stock, sugar, lemongrass and kaffir lime leaves, stirring well after each addition. Reduce the heat and simmer until the chicken is cooked through, about 15 minutes.
✦ Place in a deep serving dish and garnish with the chili "flowers" and lime slices. Serve with jasmine rice.

PER SERVING
216 calories/906 kilojoules; 24 g protein; 12 g fat, 49% of calories (3.3 g saturated, 13.7% of calories; 5.9 g monounsaturated, 24%; 2.8 g polyunsaturated, 11.3%); 4 g carbohydrate; 0.3 g dietary fiber; 373 mg sodium; 1.3 mg iron; 163 mg cholesterol.

These Buddhist temple ruins in Sukhotai date from the thirteenth century.

Curried Chicken with Lemongrass

Grilled Chicken

GAI YAHANG ESAN

SERVES 6

½ inch (1.25 cm) galangal,
  finely sliced
4 large garlic cloves, crushed
1 teaspoon salt
2 teaspoons freshly ground black
  pepper
2½ teaspoons very finely chopped
  cilantro (coriander) root
3 tablespoons freshly squeezed
  lime or lemon juice
6 chicken pieces, about 3 lb
  (1.5 kg)
cilantro (coriander) leaves, for
  garnish

From the northeast of Thailand, where the food is highly seasoned, comes this regional speciality using galangal, a more delicately flavored relative of ginger. Young fresh ginger may be substituted if galangal is unavailable.

PREPARATION *15 minutes plus 2 hours marinating time*
◆ Place the galangal, garlic, salt and pepper in a blender and chop finely. Add the lime juice, blend, then rub the mixture over the chicken. Cover with plastic wrap and refrigerate for at least 2 hours.
◆ Prepare the barbecue for cooking or preheat the broiler (grill). Brush the cooking surface of the barbecue with a little oil.

COOKING *40 minutes*
◆ Place the chicken pieces on the barbecue over medium-hot coals or under the broiler. Grill, turning occasionally, until the skin is crisp and the juices run clear when the chicken is tested with a skewer, about 15 minutes per side.
◆ Place the chicken on a serving platter and garnish with the cilantro leaves. Serve with rice and a salad.

PER SERVING
215 calories/900 kilojoules; 25 g protein; 13 g fat, 53% of calories (4.4 g saturated, 18.1% of calories; 6.4 g monounsaturated, 25.9%; 2.2 g polyunsaturated, 9%); negligible carbohydrate; negligible dietary fiber; 397 mg sodium; 1 mg iron; 83 mg cholesterol.

This gilt figure decorates the Grand Palace in Bangkok, which was built by King Rama I in the late eighteenth century.

Grilled Chicken

Southern Fried Chicken

SERVES 4

juice and grated zest of 1 lemon
1 teaspoon crushed garlic
¼ teaspoon freshly ground black
    pepper
8 skinless chicken drumsticks,
    about 4 oz (125 g) each
¼ cup (1 oz/30 g) all-purpose
    (plain) flour
1 teaspoon seasoned or lemon
    pepper
2 large eggs
1 cup (4 oz/125 g) dry bread
    crumbs
vegetable oil, for shallow-frying

Every Southern cook has her or his own way of preparing this simple but enjoyable dish. In this updated, reduced-fat version, the skin is removed from the chicken before the chicken is fried briefly in vegetable oil. The chicken is then transferred to the oven to finish cooking.

PREPARATION   *15 minutes plus*
                          30 minutes marinating time
◆ Combine the lemon juice and zest, the garlic and black pepper in a large bowl. Add the chicken and toss to coat. Cover and refrigerate for 30 minutes.
◆ Preheat the oven to 350°F (180°C).
◆ Combine the flour with the seasoned pepper and spread the mixture on a plate. Place the eggs in a shallow bowl and lightly beat with a fork. Spread the bread crumbs on a plate. First, roll the drumsticks in the flour, then dip them in the beaten eggs and finally roll them in the bread crumbs to coat.

COOKING   *45 minutes*
◆ Add enough oil to reach 1 in (2.5 cm) up the sides of a large, non-stick skillet and heat over medium heat.

Add the chicken and cook, turning occasionally, until golden on all sides, about 5 minutes. Using a slotted spoon, remove the chicken from the skillet and place on a rack in a roasting dish. Roast until the juices run clear when the chicken is tested with a skewer, about 30 minutes.
◆ Transfer the chicken to a warm serving dish and serve with a salad.

PER SERVING
*321 calories/1343 kilojoules; 29 g protein; 17 g fat,
47% of calories (4.3 g saturated, 11.8% of calories;
7 g monounsaturated, 19.3%; 5.7 g polyunsaturated, 15.9%);
13 g carbohydrate; 2.2 g dietary fiber; 200 mg sodium;
2.5 mg iron; 193 mg cholesterol.*

Barbecued Chicken

SERVES 4

SAUCE
⅓ cup (3 fl oz/90 ml) tomato
    ketchup (tomato sauce)
1 tablespoon apple cider vinegar
2 tablespoons brown sugar
2 teaspoons Worcestershire sauce
2 teaspoons American-style
    prepared mustard

1 garlic clove, finely chopped
4 chicken breast fillets, about
    4 oz (125 g) each
herb sprigs, for garnish

Long summer days and barbecues go well together, and barbecued chicken always gains wonderful flavor from the smoldering coals of an outdoor barbecue. However, pleasing results can also be achieved inside using the broiler if the weather is less than clement.

PREPARATION   *5 minutes*
◆ Combine the sauce ingredients in a small bowl.
◆ Prepare the barbecue or preheat the broiler (grill). Brush the cooking surface with a little oil.

COOKING   *25 minutes*
◆ Brush the sauce over the chicken, then place the chicken on the grill over medium-hot coals or under the broiler.
◆ Grill or broil, turning occasionally and basting with the sauce, until the chicken is cooked through, about 20 minutes.

◆ Heat any remaining sauce and spoon it over the chicken. Garnish with the herbs and serve.

PER SERVING
*199 calories/832 kilojoules; 29 g protein; 3 g fat, 13% of calories
(1 g saturated, 4.3% of calories; 1.5 g monounsaturated, 6.5%;
0.5 g polyunsaturated, 2.2%); 14 g carbohydrate; 0.7 g dietary
fiber; 375 mg sodium; 1.2 mg iron; 63 mg cholesterol.*

Barbecued Chicken

Chicken Pot Pie

Originating with the Dutch immigrants who settled Pennsylvania, this delicious hearty meal is a wonderful choice for warming up the cold winter nights. It combines savory dumplings with fresh vegetables, herbs and chicken in a well-seasoned sauce.

SERVES 6

1½ lb (750 g) boneless, skinless
    chicken thighs (thigh fillets)
2 large potatoes, diced
¾ cup (4 oz/125 g) diced carrot
⅓ cup (3 oz/90 g) diced green
    beans
2 teaspoons margarine
2 teaspoons vegetable oil
1 onion, diced
¾ cup (6 oz/180 g) corn kernels
1 chicken bouillon (stock) cube,
    crumbled
2 tablespoons chopped parsley
1 tablespoon chopped tarragon
2 teaspoons chopped sage
1 teaspoon salt
1 tablespoon cornstarch
    (cornflour)
1¾ cups (14 fl oz/440 ml)
    chicken stock, skimmed of fat
1 tablespoon light sour cream

TOPPING

½ cup (2 oz/60 g) all-purpose
    (plain) flour
½ cup (2 oz/60 g) self-rising
    (self-raising) flour
¼ teaspoon salt
¼ teaspoon freshly ground black
    pepper
3 tablespoons (1½ oz/45 g)
    margarine
¼ teaspoon dried thyme
2 tablespoons cold water

PREPARATION   *15 minutes*
✦ Dice the chicken.
✦ Preheat the oven to 400°F (200°C).

COOKING   *1 hour*
✦ Place the potato, carrot and beans in a steamer and steam together for 7 minutes, or cook in a microwave on High for 5 minutes. Set aside.
✦ Heat the margarine and oil in a wok or large skillet over medium–high heat. Add the chicken and cook in small batches until golden, about 5 minutes per batch. Using a slotted spoon, transfer to a plate.
✦ Add the onion to the wok and cook until soft, about 3 minutes.
✦ Return the chicken to the wok. Stir in the corn, crumbled bouillon cube, parsley, tarragon, sage and salt.
✦ Mix the cornstarch with the stock and add to the wok. Cook until thickened, stirring constantly, about 1 minute. Remove from the heat and stir in the sour cream and vegetables. Spoon the chicken mixture into a casserole dish.

✦ For the topping, combine the flours with the salt and pepper in a bowl. Rub the margarine in with your fingertips until the mixture resembles fine crumbs. Add the thyme. Stir in the water until a soft dough is formed.
✦ Use a teaspoon dipped in flour to scoop out small amounts of the dough. Roll these into balls. The mixture should make about 16 balls.
✦ Add the dumpling balls to the casserole dish and bake in the oven until the topping has risen and is brown in color, about 25 to 30 minutes. Serve immediately.

PER SERVING
*380 calories/1589 kilojoules; 27 g protein; 18 g fat,
41% of calories (6.1 g saturated, 13.9% of calories;
7.2 g monounsaturated, 16.4%; 4.7 g polyunsaturated, 10.7%);
29 g carbohydrate; 3.3 g dietary fiber; 882 mg sodium;
1.1 mg iron; 164 mg cholesterol.*

Chicken Pot Pie

Brunswick Stew

Brunswick stew is an all-American favorite that has been enjoyed for many generations. It was created in 1828 in Brunswick County in Virginia. Originally it was made with squirrel meat but chicken is the standard today. The beans should be soaked up to a day in advance.

SERVES 6

¾ cup (5 oz/155 g) dried cannellini beans, or 14 oz (440 g) canned cannellini beans, drained

3 cups (24 fl oz/750 ml) water

12 chicken thighs, about 4 oz (125 g) each

2 tablespoons (1 oz/30 g) butter

1 large onion, sliced

1 green bell pepper (capsicum), chopped

1 cup (8 fl oz/250 ml) chicken stock, skimmed of fat

1 chicken bouillon (stock) cube, crumbled

1¼ cups (13 oz/410 g) chopped, canned tomatoes with their juice

1 tablespoon Worcestershire sauce

1 teaspoon Tabasco sauce

1 cup (8 oz/250 g) sweet corn kernels

1 tablespoon cornstarch (cornflour)

finely chopped parsley, for garnish

herb sprigs, for garnish

PREPARATION   *1 hour plus at least 6 hours soaking time*

✦ Soak the dried beans in a large bowl containing 3 cups of the water for at least 6 hours, preferably overnight. Drain, then rinse the beans well. Place the beans in a large, heavy-bottomed saucepan with sufficient water to cover them by 3 in (7 cm).

✦ Bring the beans to a boil over medium heat, then reduce the heat and simmer, with the lid of the pot tilted to allow the steam to escape, until tender, about 45 minutes. Drain and set aside.

✦ Remove the skin and any visible fat from the chicken pieces.

The Chrysler Building—one of New York's best known landmarks.

COOKING   *1 hour*

✦ Melt the butter in a large saucepan over medium-high heat. Add the chicken in small batches and cook until browned, about 3 minutes per batch. Using a slotted spoon, transfer the chicken pieces to a plate as they are cooked.

✦ Add the onion and the bell pepper to the saucepan and cook until the onion is soft, about 3 minutes. Return the chicken to the saucepan.

✦ Stir in the stock, crumbled bouillon cube, tomatoes with their juice, Worcestershire and Tabasco sauces. Bring to a boil, then reduce the heat to low. Cover and simmer for 10 minutes.

✦ Add the corn and beans, then cover and simmer for an additional 15 minutes.

✦ Place the cornstarch in a small bowl. Gradually stir in 2 tablespoons of the cooking liquid. Add this mixture to the stew and stir constantly until the liquid has thickened, about 5 minutes.

✦ Place the stew in a deep serving bowl, garnish with the chopped parsley and herb sprigs and serve.

PER SERVING

306 calories/1281 kilojoules; 30 g protein; 10 g fat, 30% of calories (4 g saturated, 12% of calories; 4.4 g monounsaturated, 13.2%; 1.6 g polyunsaturated, 4.8%); 24 g carbohydrate; 7 g dietary fiber; 605 mg sodium; 2.4 mg iron; 168 mg cholesterol.

Creole-Style Chicken

SERVES 4

1 large onion
1 large stalk celery
2 tablespoons virgin olive oil
2 garlic cloves, crushed
8 boneless, skinless chicken
    thighs (thigh fillets), about
    2 oz (60 g) each
1¾ cups (13 oz / 410 g) chopped,
    canned tomatoes with
    their juice
⅓ cup (3 fl oz / 90 ml) dry
    vermouth or white wine
2 tablespoons brown sugar
2 tablespoons red wine vinegar
¼ teaspoon Tabasco sauce
salt, to taste
1 small red bell pepper
    (capsicum), chopped
1 small green bell pepper
    (capsicum), chopped

Creole cookery, a specialty of southern Louisiana and New Orleans in particular, is a sophisticated melding of French, Spanish, English, African and Native American influences and techniques. Tomatoes, peppers, onions, celery and hot sauce are staple ingredients in many Creole dishes.

PREPARATION   *15 minutes*
✦ Finely chop the onion and celery.

COOKING   *50 minutes*
✦ Heat the oil in a large, heavy-bottomed saucepan over medium-high heat. Add the onion, celery and garlic and cook for 2 minutes. Remove and set aside on a plate.
✦ Add the chicken and cook in 2 batches, turning occasionally, until browned, about 5 minutes per batch.
✦ Return the onion, celery, garlic and all of the chicken to the saucepan. Add the tomatoes and their juice, vermouth, sugar, vinegar, Tabasco and salt. Stir well and cover. Reduce the heat and simmer until the chicken is tender, about 20 minutes. Add the bell peppers and cook for an additional 5 minutes.
✦ Place the chicken in a deep serving bowl, spoon the sauce on top and serve.

PER SERVING
302 calories/1263 kilojoules; 25 g protein; 15 g fat, 44% of calories (3.8 g saturated, 11% of calories; 9.4 g monounsaturated, 28%; 1.8 g polyunsaturated, 5%); 15 g carbohydrate; 2.4 g dietary fiber; 253 mg sodium; 1.1 mg iron; 163 mg cholesterol.

The Mardi Gras procession in New Orleans always draws a festive crowd.

Jambalaya

SERVES 6

8 oz (250 g) cooked shrimp
(prawns)
1 cooked chicken, about
3 lb (1.5 kg)
4 slices (rashers) lean bacon,
chopped
2 teaspoons vegetable oil
1 large onion, chopped
2 stalks celery, chopped
1½ cups (10½ oz/330 g) long-
grain rice
2 cups (16 fl oz/500 ml)
chicken stock, skimmed of fat
½ teaspoon salt
¼ teaspoon black pepper
¼ teaspoon cayenne pepper
1 bay leaf
1 small green bell pepper
(capsicum), chopped
1 small red bell pepper
(capsicum), chopped
1¾ cups (13 oz/410 g) chopped,
canned tomatoes with
their juice
1 tablespoon chopped parsley

The city of New Orleans was founded by the French and then later ruled by the Spanish; its cuisine reveals the influences of both countries. This classic dish is related to the Spanish dish, paella. Jambalaya is one of Creole cuisine's most famous dishes.

PREPARATION   15 minutes
◆ Shell and devein the shrimp.
◆ Remove the skin from the chicken, take the meat off the bone and cut into bite-sized pieces.

COOKING   35 minutes
◆ Place the bacon in a medium-sized, non-stick skillet and cook over medium-high heat until crisp, about 5 minutes. Transfer to a plate lined with paper towels to drain.
◆ Heat the oil in a large saucepan over medium heat. Add the onion and cook until soft, about 3 minutes. Add the celery and rice and cook, stirring continuously, until the rice is coated with the oil, about 3 minutes.
◆ Pour in the stock, add the seasonings and the bay leaf and bring to a boil. Reduce the heat, cover and simmer for 10 minutes.

◆ Add the bell peppers, tomatoes and their juice and continue to simmer, covered, for 5 minutes.
◆ Stir in the shrimp, chicken and bacon. Cook until heated through and the rice is cooked, about 5 minutes. Remove the bay leaf.
◆ Transfer to a warm serving dish, sprinkle with the parsley and serve immediately.

PER SERVING
*464 calories/1943 kilojoules; 48 g protein; 10 g fat,
14% of calories (3.1 g saturated, 4.3% of calories;
4.2 g monounsaturated, 5.9%; 2.7 g polyunsaturated, 3.8%);
45 g carbohydrate; 2.7 g dietary fiber; 1068 mg sodium;
3.3 mg iron; 192 mg cholesterol.*

A delicatessen specializing in Cajun foods. Cajun cooking is related to French cuisine, but it is more robust.

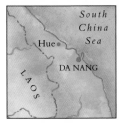

Curried Chicken with Rice Noodles

GA NAU CARI NUOC DUA

SERVES 6

1 lb (500 g) chicken breast fillets
4 waxy potatoes
2 oz (60 g) rice noodles (rice
  vermicelli)
2 tablespoons vegetable oil
1 large onion, finely chopped
2 garlic cloves, finely chopped
2 tablespoons mild curry powder
1 stalk lemongrass, thinly sliced
2 cups (16 fl oz/500 ml)
  coconut milk
1 teaspoon salt
bean sprouts, for garnish
1 teaspoon finely chopped red
  chili, for garnish

With its delicious creamy sauce, this dish resembles a chunky soup. The ingredients reflect the variety of foreign influences that have shaped Vietnam's cuisine: potatoes were introduced by the French; coconut milk by the Malaysians.

PREPARATION   *10 minutes*
✦ Cut the chicken into bite-sized pieces.
✦ Partly cook the potatoes in the microwave on High for about 5 minutes, or steam for 7 minutes. Then dice the potatoes.
✦ Bring a large saucepan of water to a boil. Add the noodles and cook until just tender, about 2 minutes.

COOKING   *30 minutes*
✦ Heat the oil in a large saucepan over medium heat. Add the onion and garlic and cook, stirring, until the onion is soft, about 3 minutes. Stir in the curry powder and cook for 1 minute. Add the chicken, potatoes, lemongrass, coconut milk and salt. Bring to a boil,

reduce the heat and simmer until the chicken is tender, about 15 minutes. Add the noodles and cook for 1 minute.
✦ Place the chicken, noodles and sauce in a serving bowl, sprinkle the bean sprouts and chili on top and serve with fresh crusty rolls.

PER SERVING
369 calories/1544 kilojoules; 24 g protein; 19 g fat,
47% of calories (12.6 g saturated, 31% of calories;
2.4 g monounsaturated, 6.1%; 4 g polyunsaturated, 9.9%);
25 g carbohydrate; 2.1 g dietary fiber; 411 mg sodium;
5.3 mg iron; 42 mg cholesterol.

Chicken and Lemongrass

GA XAO XA OT

SERVES 4

4 stalks lemongrass
1 small red chili
1 tablespoon vegetable oil
1 large onion, sliced
3 garlic cloves, finely chopped
8 skinless chicken drumsticks,
  about 4 oz (125 g) each
3 tablespoons fish sauce
1 teaspoon soy sauce
2 teaspoons sugar
1 cup (8 fl oz/250 ml) water
herb sprigs, for garnish

Lemongrass, a long aromatic grass with a slightly bulbous base, is an important herb in both Vietnamese and Thai cooking. Only the tender, bulbous base of the stalk is used. Lemongrass is also a natural insect repellent.

PREPARATION   *10 minutes*
✦ Place the lemongrass and chili in a blender and chop finely.

COOKING   *30 minutes*
✦ Heat the oil in a large, non-stick skillet over medium heat. Add the onion and garlic and cook until the onion is soft, about 3 minutes. Add the lemongrass and chili mixture and cook for 1 minute.
✦ Add the chicken, fish sauce, soy sauce and sugar. Mix well. Add the water, reduce the heat and simmer until the chicken is cooked through, about 20 minutes.

Using a slotted spoon, transfer the chicken to a warm serving dish and spoon the cooking juices on top.
✦ Garnish with the herb sprigs and serve with rice.

PER SERVING
233 calories/975 kilojoules; 27 g protein; 12 g fat, 47% of calories
(3.2 g saturated, 12% of calories; 4.5 g monounsaturated, 18%); 4.3
g polyunsaturated, 17 %); 5 g carbohydrate; 0.9 g dietary fiber;
294 mg sodium; 1.9 mg iron; 103 mg cholesterol.

Sweet-and-Sour Chicken

CHIEN CHUA NGOT

This sweet-and-sour dish is colorful and full of fresh vegetables. Vietnamese cooking has been strongly influenced by that of China, but you will find that this is lighter in flavor and texture than Chinese sweet-and-sour dishes.

SERVES 4

SAUCE

2 tablespoons white wine vinegar
1 tablespoon soy sauce
2 tablespoons sugar
1 tablespoon oyster sauce
1 teaspoon sesame oil
2 tablespoons cornstarch
  (cornflour)
1 cup (8 fl oz / 250 ml) water

2 small vine-ripened tomatoes
1 lb (500 g) chicken breast fillets
1 in (2.5 cm) ginger
2 tablespoons, plus 2 teaspoons
  vegetable oil
1 onion, sliced
2 garlic cloves, finely chopped
1 carrot, cut into julienne strips
1 stalk celery, sliced diagonally
5 small pickled onions, sliced
4 scallions (spring onions),
  sliced diagonally
1 cucumber, diced

PREPARATION   *20 minutes*
◆ Mix all the sauce ingredients in a bowl.
◆ Place the tomatoes in a bowl and cover with boiling water. Let stand until the skin begins to split, about 10 minutes. Remove the tomatoes from the water, peel and chop.
◆ Cut the chicken into bite-sized cubes.
◆ Peel and grate the ginger.

COOKING   *25 minutes*
◆ Heat 2 tablespoons of the oil in a wok or large skillet over medium-high heat. Add the chicken in 2 batches and stir-fry until cooked through, about 5 minutes per batch. Remove from the wok and set aside.

◆ Add the remaining oil to the wok. Add the onion, garlic and ginger and stir-fry until the onion is soft, about 3 minutes. Add the carrot and celery and cook for 1 minute. Add the tomatoes, pickled onions, scallions and cucumber and cook for 2 minutes. Remove from the wok and set aside.
◆ Pour the sauce mixture into the wok and cook, stirring, until thickened, about 3 minutes. Return the chicken and vegetables to the wok and stir until heated through, about 3 minutes.
◆ Transfer to a deep serving dish and serve with boiled rice.

PER SERVING
295 calories/1235 kilojoules; 30 g protein; 11 g fat, 35% of calories (1.9 g saturated, 6% of calories; 2.8 g monounsaturated, 9%; 6.3 g polyunsaturated, 20%); 17 g carbohydrate; 2.7 g dietary fiber; 573 mg sodium; 1.5 mg iron; 63 mg cholesterol.

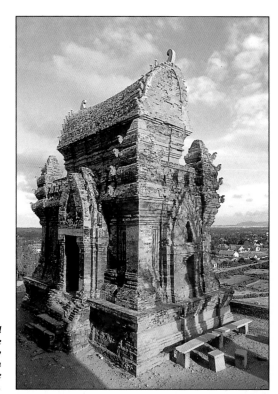

This well-weathered Vietnamese shrine contrasts sharply with the modern architecture of the houses below.

Sweet-and-Sour Chicken

Special Ingredients

BASIL

Basil is an annual herb with aromatic leaves that add a distinctive flavor to many dishes. It is thought to have grown first in tropical Asia and Africa and was known in ancient Egypt, Rome and Greece. There are a number of varieties of basil available today. Sweet basil is used in Mediterranean cuisine, while the main varieties used in Thai (as well as Laotian and Vietnamese) cooking are hot basil, also known as holy or heavenly basil or hairy basil, and purple basil which has the fragrance of cloves. If hairy or purple basil are not available, sweet basil may be used. Although dried basil is available, fresh leaves have a sweet pungent flavor and should be used when possible.

BANANA LEAVES

Banana leaves are widely used in the cooking of Southeast Asia, the Caribbean, Mexico, and Central and South America. As they are pliable, they are ideal for dishes which require food to be wrapped. Meat, vegetables, and sometimes dessert foods, are wrapped in leaves and the parcels tied with raffia or twine, or secured with toothpicks, before being steamed. Banana leaves are available from specialty Asian food stores. If they are unavailable, aluminum foil can be substituted; however, as banana leaves are porous, they allow the steam to penetrate more efficiently. Although the leaves are not eaten, they impart a subtle fragrance to food, and give a special touch to the presentation of any dish.

BAY LEAVES

The bay tree *(Laurus nobilis)* can grow to 50 feet (15 meters) given its preferred dry Mediterranean-type climate.

Bay leaves

Its aromatic leaves are one of the most popular herbs for cooking, however, they should be used sparingly as they impart a strong savory flavor. Bay leaves are available fresh and dried and are used to enhance marinades, pâtés and casseroles, particularly those made of lamb and beef. Whole bay leaves are often added to a dish while it is cooking, and then removed before it is served, and they are an essential component of a bouquet garni.

BOUQUET GARNI

A bouquet garni is a bundle of either fresh or dried herbs and/or spices used to add flavor to stocks, soups and slow-cooking dishes such as stews without the herbs dispersing throughout the liquid. The bouquet garni makes it easy to remove the herbs before serving. When fresh herbs are used, they can be tied together by their stalks, with cooking twine or thread, or the herbs are wrapped up with the stalks of a flavorsome vegetable such as celery or leek. In the case of a bouquet garni made from dried herbs, their leaves are enclosed in a square of cheesecloth and secured with thread. The traditional bouquet garni combination is parsley, bay leaves and thyme but,

Bouquet garni

depending on the type of dish being cooked, other herbs, spices or vegetables can be used. They can be easily prepared at home, but the dried herb variety is available from specialty food stores.

CANDLENUTS

Known as *kemiri* in Indonesia, and *buah keras* (hard shell) in Malaysia, candlenuts come from the candleberry tree *(Aleurites moluccana)* which is native to eastern Asia and some of the Pacific Islands. Originally introduced to Hawaii by the Polynesians, it is now an important element of the vegetation there. At one time the people of what is now known as Indonesia burned the kernels of these nuts, using them as a primitive type of candle; hence the name, "candlenuts." They are also known as Indian walnuts. Candlenuts are used to thicken and flavor curries in Indonesia. They are also a good energy source, and in some areas, particularly Java, they are roasted for eating. Candlenuts are often sold at Asian food stores; brazil or macadamia nuts can be used as substitutes if necessary. Candlenuts should be stored in a cool, dry place in a container with a tight-fitting lid. In these conditions they will keep for some months.

Candlenuts

CHORIZO

This spicy, dry sausage was first made in Spain, where it comes in many different varieties. All chorizos contain pork. Hanging in a fifteenth-century Spanish kitchen, they would attest to the owner's Christianity, serving as visual proof to the Inquisition that no one of the Jewish or Muslim faith lived there. In addition to pork, another essential ingredient of chorizo is paprika, sweet or spicy, although other minced meats and seasonings may be added as well. Spanish chorizo is made with smoked pork whereas Mexican chorizo is made with fresh. Chorizo contains very little fat and can be eaten raw, thinly sliced and served with bread, wine and olives. It can also be broiled (grilled), fried or either cut into chunks or crumbled and simmered in casseroles and soups or stews. Remove the casing from the sausage before using. Chorizo can be purchased from most specialty food stores and some supermarkets.

Chorizo

CIDER

Cider is made from the pressed juice of apples (or occasionally pears). Sweet cider is non-alcoholic and is drunk straight or diluted with water. Hard, or fermented, cider is an alcoholic beverage, popular in Britain and northern France since Celtic times. Cider may be fermented naturally or through the addition of yeast and can vary greatly in alcoholic strength. Often filtered after fermentation, the resulting liquid is a clear, golden yellow color which is then bottled. Cider is available as a still drink but can also be carbonated to make it sparkling. Apart from being prized as drinks, sweet and hard cider have a long tradition of being added to sauces, desserts and dishes including chicken and pork. Once opened, cider should be stored in the refrigerator, and treated as any other drink.

COCONUT

The coconut is the fruit of the coconut palm *(Cocus nucifera)* which is native to the tropics. Both the soft white flesh of the nut and the clear juice or "water" in the center of the nut are used in cooking. The flesh is available packaged in cans or plastic packets, sweetened or unsweetened, or shredded or desiccated. Powdered coconut and coconut paste are also available from specialty Asian food stores. The juice can be bought canned or frozen. Shredded coconut is used plain or toasted as a garnish or it can be used in sweet or savory dishes. Coconut milk and coconut cream are the liquids obtained from coconut flesh after simmering it in boiling water or milk. They can also be made from desiccated or powdered coconut and are also sold in cartons and cans.

COUSCOUS

Couscous is made from semolina, which is coarsely ground durum wheat. The grains of semolina are sprinkled with flour and water, then rubbed, either by hand or machine, into tiny pellets. Couscous was made in the deserts of North Africa for centuries by the Berber tribes, though they originally used millet, not wheat. Couscous may be steamed over water and served like pasta as an accompaniment to other main dishes, or it can be mixed with honey, fruit or nuts and served as a dessert. While couscous is still made by hand in North Africa, and this handmade variety can be bought from some gourmet or Middle Eastern food stores, the machine-made variety is more readily available. Packaged precooked couscous is also available.

Couscous

CUMIN

Cumin's long seeds are quite strongly scented and have a spicy, slightly bitter taste. *Cuminum cyminum* is an annual herb native to the Mediterranean region, and was known to the people there from ancient times. Cumin seeds can be used whole or ground, and are essential in curry powders and Mexican chili powders. It is very popular in the cuisines of Mexico, India and North Africa. Cumin is also a popular pickling spice. Both the seeds and the powder are generally available in supermarkets.

Cumin

EDIBLE FLOWERS

Many flowers are attractive and delicious in salads and as garnishes. It is safer to buy edible flowers from specialty food stores or to pick your own from the garden. Do not use flowers that have been sprayed with pesticides and check that a particular flower is not poisonous before using it. Flowers that are commonly used include pansies, violas, nasturtiums, carnations, roses, lilacs, borage, chive flowers, marigolds and orange blossoms.

FISH SAUCE

Fish sauce is indispensable to many Southeast Asian cuisines. It is made by placing salted small fish such as anchovies, or shellfish such as shrimp, in jars or barrels and allowing them to ferment over a few months. The resulting liquid—fish sauce—is collected, strained and then bottled. The concentrated fish left after the liquid has been drawn off is used in fish dishes for a stronger flavor. Varying in color from golden to dark brown, fish sauce is known by different names in different countries; for example, *nam pla* in Thailand, and *nuoc cham* or *nuoc mam* in Vietnam, Laos and Kampuchea. Used as a condiment in a similar manner to soy sauce, there is no substitute for its distinctive salty flavor. Look for fish sauce in Asian food stores. Once opened, it will keep for several months in the refrigerator.

GALANGAL

Galangal *(Alpinia galangal)* is known as *kha* in Thailand and *laos* in Indonesia. Native to Southeast Asia and China, this semitropical plant has been used as an herb for at least one thousand years. Deep buff colored and smooth skinned, galangal resembles ginger but is more delicate and fragrant in flavor. It is used extensively in Southeast Asian and Indian cooking. Galangal is sold by Asian food stores and some supermarkets. If fresh galangal is unavailable, dried or preserved galangal may be substituted. Dried galangal has to be reconstituted in hot water for one hour before using. Powdered galangal is also available.

Galangal

GHEE

Ghee has been used in Indian cooking for well over 2000 years. It is also used in Asian cooking, although in some countries the ghee is made from the milk of the water buffalo rather than the cow. Ghee is a type of clarified butter and is ideal for sautéeing and frying. It imparts a lovely color and flavor to cooked food. It is available from specialty food stores and some supermarkets. Ghee can be frozen for up to one year or stored, tightly wrapped, in the refrigerator for up to 6 months. If butter is used in a recipe instead of ghee, it will need to be clarified. To clarify, melt the butter in a saucepan over low heat. When the butter is simmering, continually skim the froth from the surface until only clear liquid remains, about 5 minutes.

GINGER

Originally a native of Asia, the ginger plant *(Zingiber officinale)* is now grown throughout the world's tropical regions. Ginger is the plant's root or rhizome and was one of the earliest spices taken to Europe, and now is used there in drinks, such as ginger ale, in cakes, and is preserved in syrup or sugar. In Asia ginger is also an important spice. It is one of the basic ingredients of curries, and eaten freshly grated, cooked and crystallized. It is found in many forms: fresh, powdered, dried, crystallized and preserved. All these will last indefinitely, except for fresh ginger, which will keep for up to 2 months if stored in a cool place.

KEFALOTIRI

Kefalotiri is a hard, salty Greek cheese traditionally made from ewe's milk, but today cow's milk or a mixture of the two milks is more commonly used. Pale yellow in color, it gets its name from the Greek word for head—*kefali*—because the cheese is pressed into a head-shaped mold. It is then salted and allowed to mature. Similar to Parmesan, kefalotiri is mostly used for grating and cooking. It is sold by specialty food stores. Kefalotiri should be stored in an airtight container in the refrigerator.

Ginger

Kefalotiri

LEMONGRASS

Also known as citronella, lemongrass is an aromatic herb that grows in most tropical countries. The lower, more tender part of the stem is pounded to release its strong lemon flavor. This is then added to a dish to give it the sharp freshness that is so characteristic of Thai and other Asian cuisines. Its bulbous base is cut up and used in curries. Lemongrass can be bought in jars, dried or in powdered form, but the flavor is not as intense as the fresh lemongrass stalks which are readily available from Asian food stores. The fresh stalks should be kept in the refrigerator.

LENTILS AND OTHER PULSES

Pulses are the dried seeds of legumes, of which there are hundreds of species. Some of the most popular pulses include soybeans, dried split peas and beans, urad dal and chana dal from India and lentils. Lentils, for example, vary in color from green to brown to bright orange. They have been cultivated since ancient times in places as far apart as

Lentils

Switzerland and China. An excellent source of vegetable protein and some of the B vitamins, pulses have long been a staple part of the diet of people with limited access to meat and fish and are also popular with vegetarians. Pulses are most frequently used in soups and stews and of course in dal from India. Most pulses are readily available though some, such as chana dal and urad dal, may have to be purchased from specialty food stores. Stored in a cool, dark place, pulses will keep indefinitely.

MUSTARD

Mustard is made from the seeds of annual plants belonging to the cabbage family. There are three varieties of seed: black (which is spicy), brown (less so), and white (which is more bitter and pungent). The seeds are crushed and then mixed with water or vinegar to produce a sharp pungent condiment. Jean Naigeon, an eighteenth-century French merchant, created the famous Dijon mustard by mixing black and brown seeds with the unfermented juice of grapes (verjuice). French and American mustards are usually milder than the hot English variety. Most mustards are sold as ready-made pastes, although hot English mustard is available in a powdered form. Mustard is now available in many exotic flavors as its popularity has grown. Store mustard pastes in the refrigerator and powders in a cool, dark cupboard.

Mustard

OKRA

Okra is the green pod or fruit of the herb *Abelmoschus esculentus*. It is one of the essential ingredients of Greek, Middle Eastern, Cajun, Caribbean and South American cooking. Okra is also known as ladies' fingers, bamia and gumbo. It is best used when very young, before the seeds are completely formed. The pods, cooked whole or sliced, impart a distinctive flavor as well as a gelatinous texture, which makes them an excellent addition to soups and casseroles. They can also be steamed, sautéed, braised, used in salads or as an accompaniment to rice or meat dishes.

OLIVES

The olive *(Olea europea)* and its oil has played an important role in shaping the cuisine of Mediterranean countries for a very long time. All fresh olives, whether green or black, have an intensely bitter flesh and need processing before they become edible. Varying in color, size and shape, olives are prepared in a variety of ways. The popular Greek kalamata olive is soaked in a solution containing vinegar which gives it its distinctive flavor. Spanish-style olives are soaked in brine for up to 12 months, with sugar added to aid fermentation. They are sometimes pitted, then stuffed with such ingredients as pimiento, onion or jalapeño pepper. Olives are versatile and can be eaten on their own or used in cooking.

ONIONS

The onion *(Allium cepa)* is a biennial member of the lily family. Several varieties are available, differing in size, color and pungency. Onions can be gently browned in oil and used as the basis of a casserole; or can be braised, boiled, stuffed, added to sauces or used as a garnish, either raw or cooked. The small red onion is popular in Mediterranean and North African cooking, and being sweeter-tasting and more juicy than the more common, large yellow or brown onion, it is used as often raw as it is cooked. The larger red onion, also mild enough to be eaten raw, is widely available and is a good substitute for the small red onion if it is unavailable. Fresh onions should be kept in a well-ventilated, cool spot where they should remain in good condition for up to one month.

Red onion

PARSLEY

Parsley is a biennial plant that has been widely used for centuries. It was popular with the ancient Greeks and Romans, who used it for medicinal purposes as well as in the kitchen. In the seventeenth century it was taken to America by British colonists. Today parsley is one of the most widely grown and used herbs. Rich in vitamins A, B and especially C, parsley enhances other flavors and is one of the main components of a bouquet garni. It complements just about every savory dish and makes an attractive garnish. It is also used in marinades, stocks, soups, sauces and vinaigrettes, and can be added to butter to make a delicious spread. The most popular varieties of parsley are the curly-leaf and flat-leaf (or Italian) types. Curly-leaf parsley is excellent

Parsley

for garnishing and salads while the stronger flavored flat-leaf parsley is good for cooking. Parsley can easily be grown in a garden or in a pot on a sunny window ledge. Fresh parsley is best stored in the refrigerator, either with its stems in water or wrapped in plastic and stored in the salad crisper.

PEANUTS

The peanut is really a legume, although it is generally thought of as a nut. It grows underground on the roots of *Arachis hypogaea,* in a way that is similar to how potatoes grow. The outer shell of the peanut is actually the dried pod of the plant. Also known as the groundnut or monkey nut, the plant is native to Brazil and now thrives in many tropical countries, especially India and parts of China.

Peanuts have been found in tombs almost 3000 years old. The nuts can be eaten raw or roasted, and are rich in protein and high in monounsaturated oil. This oil is extracted and sold as peanut or groundnut oil, and is widely used in cooking and salad dressings. If peanuts are to be kept for a long time, they are best bought in the shell. Discard any moldy peanuts— they may be toxic.

Peanuts

RICE WINE

The taste and golden color of Chinese rice wine *(shao hsing)* is reminiscent of malt whiskey. The preparation and making of rice wine in China has been recorded since the time of Confucius. A vital ingredient in many Chinese dishes, rice wine is also used as a marinade and is added to stir-fry recipes. Chinese rice wine is also drunk warm as an accompaniment to meals. Stored in a cool, dark place, it will keep for a long period of time, but its flavor will lessen with age.

SAFFRON

Saffron is made from the dried stigmas of the autumn-flowering crocus *(Crocus sativus).* The flowers have to be picked by hand and as about 150,000 flowers are needed to obtain 2 pounds (1 kilogram) of saffron, it is clearly the most expensive spice in the world. The plant originated in Asia Minor and was later taken to the Mediterranean region and now Spain is the world's major producer. Saffron has always been used in cooking, but in ancient times it was also extensively used for medicinal purposes and as a clothing dye. However, it is now much too expensive for this, although in India it is sometimes still used to dye the veil of a bride. Saffron is intensely aromatic, with a slightly pungent flavor, and gives a beautiful yellow color to any dish to which it is added. It is available in powdered form as well, though the powder is considered inferior in flavor to the threads. It should be used sparingly and stored in an airtight container.

Saffron

SAMBAL ULEK (SAMBAL BAJAK)

This Indonesian chili sauce is widely used in Indonesia, Malaysia and southern India as a seasoning and served with a variety of curries and rice dishes either as a condiment or a side dish. It is usually made from a base of chilies ground in a stone pestle called a ulekan. Sambal ulek is available in glass jars from specialty food stores and can be kept in the refrigerator for several months.

SANSHO PEPPER

Sansho pepper is a Japanese spice which is usually sprinkled on chicken dishes, noodles and soups, giving them a mildly hot and citrus flavor. The leaves of the prickly ash tree *(Zanthoxylum piperitum)* are dried and ground to make the greenish brown spice which is also used in the Japanese seven-spice blend known as *shichimi togarashi.* Sansho pepper can be bought from Asian food stores and should be stored in an airtight container. It is best to buy it in small quantities as it loses its flavor quickly. The pepper should be used sparingly, otherwise it overwhelms other flavors.

SHALLOTS (FRENCH SHALLOTS)

The shallot is similar in taste to both onion and garlic. Somewhat larger than garlic and being a member of the *Allium* genus, it also forms a bulb, but its tough outer skin is deep golden brown in color. Greatly favored in traditional French cuisine, the shallot also features prominently in the cooking of China, Vietnam and the Indian subcontinent. It is particularly useful for flavoring sauces such as béarnaise, red wine and white sauces, because the shallot will emulsify more easily than onions. It is a good choice for salads and as a complement to lighter flavored foods such as fish and chicken. Keep shallots in a well-ventilated place, but not in the refrigerator as other foods may absorb their flavor. Be sure when buying the shallots that they are plump and firm.

Shallots

SHIITAKE MUSHROOMS

Shiitake mushrooms are native to Japan and Korea. Their name is derived from the *shii* tree, one of the trees on which they grow; but they also grow on other trees, such as oaks—in California they are commonly called golden oak mushrooms. These versatile, dark-capped mushrooms with pale gills taste somewhat different to Western mushrooms. They are also larger, juicier and very intense in flavor. They are a common ingredient in Japanese cooking. Dried shiitakes can be found in most Asian food stores. Dried shiitakes should be soaked in either hot water for 30 minutes or, if preferred, in cold water for several hours, prior to using them in a recipe. Stored in an airtight container, dried mushrooms will keep for up to one year.

Shiitake mushrooms

SZECHUAN PEPPER

This mildly hot spice comes from the prickly ash tree *(Zanthoxylum piperitum)* and is named after its Chinese province of origin. Also known as Chinese pepper, it is available from Asian food stores in whole or powdered form. The whole berries are heated then ground to produce the powder. Szechuan pepper is sprinkled over grilled chicken and fish to give them a distinctive peppery-lemony flavor and aroma.

TOMATILLOS

Tomatillos *(Physalis ixocarpa)* are small, green tomato-like vegetables which are covered with a papery husk. Also called Mexican green tomatoes, they belong to the tomato family and are related to the cape gooseberry. In fact, if tomatillos are unavailable, cooked cape gooseberries can be used instead as long as they are a minor ingredient in the recipe. Tomatillos are not usually eaten raw. Before cooking, the husk must be removed and the fruit washed. Their tart flavor makes tomatillos perfect for green sauces for dishes from Mexico and the American Southwest. Tomatillos are available fresh from specialty food stores (choose bright green, firm ones) or canned from most supermarkets. Fresh tomatillos can be stored in a paper bag in the refrigerator for up to one month.

WASABI

Wasabi is made from the root of *Wasabia japonica,* a plant native to Japan and similar to the horseradish root. The root has a brown skin and pale green flesh and its flavor is less pungent than horseradish. Hotter than even the hottest chilies, wasabi is served sparingly as a condiment with a number of Japanese dishes. The Japanese pickle, *wasabi-zuke,* is made by pickling wasabi in sake. To prepare fresh wasabi for use as a condiment, peel and grate the root. Although the fresh root is not readily available in Western countries, wasabi is usually available in both paste (in tubes) and powdered forms from Asian grocery stores. Mix powdered wasabi with a little cold water and leave for about 10 minutes before using to allow the flavor to develop; it should not be made further in advance or it will lose its heat. Store wasabi paste in the refrigerator once opened. The powder should be stored in a container with a tight-fitting lid in a cool, dry place.

Wasabi

Index